JOEL HORWOOD

Joel Horwood is a playwright, director and dramaturg. His work in theatre includes Fringe First Award-winning *Food* (The Imaginary Body); *Stoopud Fucken Animals* (Traverse Theatre); *I Caught Crabs in Walberswick*, *I ♥ Peterborough* (Eastern Angles); *A Series of Increasingly Impossible Acts* (for Secret Theatre at the Lyric Hammersmith); *I Want My Hat Back* (National Theatre, nominated for the Best Family and Entertainment Show Olivier Award); *This Changes Everything* (Tonic Theatre, nominated for Best New Play at the Writer's Guild Awards); *The Little Matchgirl and Happier Tales* (Shakespeare's Globe); *Berberian Sound Studio* (Donmar Warehouse); *The Great Elephant Chase* (Burgtheater, Vienna); *The Ocean at the End of the Lane* (National Theatre, nominated for Best New Play at the Olivier and WhatsOnStage Awards); and *The Great Gatsby* (Uppsala Stadsteater).

Other Adaptations in this Series

ANIMAL FARM
Ian Wooldridge
Adapted from George Orwell

ANNA KARENINA
Helen Edmundson
Adapted from Leo Tolstoy

ARABIAN NIGHTS
Dominic Cooke

THE ASSASSINATION OF
  MARGARET THATCHER
Alexandra Wood
Adapted from Hilary Mantel

AROUND THE WORLD IN 80 DAYS
Laura Eason
Adapted from Jules Verne

THE BEEKEEPER OF ALEPPO
Nesrin Alrefaai and Matthew Spangler
Adapted from Christy Lefteri

THE CANTERBURY TALES
Mike Poulton
Adapted from Geoffrey Chaucer

A CHRISTMAS CAROL
Karen Louise Hebden
Adapted from Charles Dickens

CORAM BOY
Helen Edmundson
Adapted from Jamila Gavin

DANCE OF DEATH
Richard Eyre
Adapted from August Strindberg

DAVID COPPERFIELD
Alastair Cording
Adapted from Charles Dickens

DR JEKYLL AND MR HYDE
David Edgar
Adapted from Robert Louis Stevenson

DRACULA: THE BLOODY TRUTH
John Nicholson and Le Navet Bete
Adapted from Bram Stoker

EMMA
Martin Millar and Doon MacKichan
Adapted from Jane Austen

FAR FROM THE MADDING CROWD
Mark Healy
Adapted from Thomas Hardy

FRANKENSTEIN
Patrick Sandford
Adapted from Mary Shelley

GREAT EXPECTATIONS
Nick Ormerod and Declan Donnellan
Adapted from Charles Dickens

GRIMM TALES
Philip Wilson
Adapted from Philip Pullman

THE HAUNTING
Hugh Janes
Adapted from Charles Dickens

HIS DARK MATERIALS
Nicholas Wright
Adapted from Philip Pullman

JANE EYRE
Chris Bush
Adapted from Charlotte Brontë

THE JUNGLE BOOK
Stuart Paterson
Adapted from Rudyard Kipling

KENSUKE'S KINGDOM
Stuart Paterson
Adapted from Michael Morpurgo

KES
Lawrence Till
Adapted from Barry Hines

KING ARTHUR
John Nicholson and Le Navet Bete

THE MANNINGTREE WITCHES
Ava Pickett
Adapted from A. K. Blakemore

THE MASSIVE TRAGEDY OF
  MADAME BOVARY
John Nicholson and Javier Marzan
Adapted from Gustave Flaubert

NOUGHTS & CROSSES
Dominic Cooke
Adapted from Malorie Blackman

THE RAGGED TROUSERED
  PHILANTHROPISTS
Howard Brenton
Adapted from Robert Tressell

THE RAILWAY CHILDREN
Mike Kenny
Adapted from E. Nesbit

SUMMERFOLK
Nina Raine and Moses Raine
Adapted from Maxim Gorky

SWALLOWS AND AMAZONS
Helen Edmundson and Neil Hannon
Adapted from Arthur Ransome

THE THREE MUSKETEERS
John Nicholson and Le Navet Bete
Adapted from Alexandre Dumas

THE TIME MACHINE: A COMEDY
Steven Canny and John Nicholson
Adapted from H.G. Wells

TREASURE ISLAND
John Nicholson and Le Navet Bete
Adapted from Robert Louis Stevenson

THE WAVES
Flora Wilson Brown
Adapted from Virginia Woolf

Joel Horwood

SHERLOCK HOLMES

And the Threat from Within

NICK HERN BOOKS

London
www.nickhernbooks.co.uk

A Nick Hern Book

Sherlock Holmes first published in Great Britain as a paperback original in 2026 by Nick Hern Books Limited, The Glasshouse, 49a Goldhawk Road, London W12 8QP

Sherlock Holmes copyright © 2026 Joel Horwood

Joel Horwood has asserted his right to be identified as the author of this work

Cover design by FEAST; photography by Rich Southgate

Designed and typeset by Nick Hern Books, London
Printed in Great Britain by Mimeo Ltd, Huntingdon, Cambridgeshire PE29 6XX

A CIP catalogue record for this book is available from the British Library

ISBN 978 1 83904 596 7

www.nickhernbooks.co.uk/environmental-policy

Nick Hern Books' authorised representative in the EU is
Easy Access System Europe – Mustamäe tee 50, 10621 Tallinn, Estonia
email gpsr.requests@easproject.com

*For the migrants, refugees and immigrants of London –
past and present – whose lives, labour, histories and hopes
continue to make this city possible.*

And my pal Danny.

Sherlock Holmes was commissioned by and first produced and performed at Regent's Park Open Air Theatre, London, on 13 May 2026 (previews from 2 May), with the following cast:

SHOLTO/JUDGE	Christopher Akrill
POCKETS/REFEREE	Andre Antonio
SMALL/LESTRADE	Will Brown
GRAZIANO/BILL	Paolo Guidi
MORSTAN	Benjamin Harrold
SHERLOCK HOLMES	Joshua James
WATSON	Jyuddah Jaymes
MARY	Nadi Kemp-Sayfi
MRS HUDSON/LUCIA	Marcia Lecky
TONGA/AZAD	Mervin Noronha
LIN/NANCY	Yuyu Rau
DOMINGO	Theo Reece
ALEKSANDRA/ PADSHAH BEGUM JAHAN	Rakhee Sharma
SLIP JENNY/SINGER	Tamara Tare
MYCROFT/THADDEUS	Patrick Warner

All other roles played by the company

Co-Costume Designer & Supervisor	Lisa Aitken
Composer	Jherek Bischoff
Movement Director	Charlotte Broom
Casting Director	Stuart Burt CDG, CSA
Associate Director	Nathanael Campbell
Lighting Designer	Ryan Day
Associate Sound Designer	Niamh Gaffney
Wigs, Hair & Make-up Designer & Supervisor	Carole Hancock
Voice & Dialect Coaches	Hazel Holder & Gurkiran Kaur

Director	Sean Holmes
Writer	Joel Horwood
Intimacy Support	Ingrid Mackinnon
Casting Associate	Peter Noden
Fight Director	Enric Ortuño
Sound Designer	Elena Peña
Set & Co-Costume Designer	Grace Smart

Hindustani & Punjabi Translator   Rakhee Sharma
All other translations by the company

'We shouldn't apologise for our past, let alone be discussing reparations… Young people can no longer be taught to dislike our country and our history so much that they wouldn't fight for it. Every single second that we spend on these matters is a second lost while our adversaries are advancing.'

Kemi Badenoch, speech on foreign policy, Conservative Party, 25 February 2025

Characters

221B Baker Street
SHERLOCK HOLMES
DR JOHN WATSON
MRS HUDSON

MARY

India, 1857
TONGA / AZAD
PRIVATE SMALL
CAPTAIN MORSTAN
SIR CHARLES SHOLTO

Pondicherry Lodge
THADDEUS SHOLTO
WILLIAMS

The Law
INSPECTOR LESTRADE
POLICE OFFICER
JUDGE

Baker Street Irregulars
LUCIA
POCKETS
SLY SYD
JEAN
TOMMO
SLIP JENNY
NANCY

The Jade Dragon
LIN
BILL

The Diogenes Club
MYCROFT HOLMES
SECURITY PERSONNEL

The Archive
ARTHUR CADOGAN-
 WEST

The Wonders of the Empire
DOOR LADY
RINGMASTER
AUDREY
DOMINGO
POGO THE CLOWN
JUGGLER
SINGER

Tower Bridge
PADSHAH BEGUM JAHAN

Other Londoners
REFEREE
ENZO 'BRICK JAW'
 GRAZIANO
ALEKSANDRA
CONDUCTOR
CELLMATE
DRIVER

Chorus
CROWDS
POLICE
SERVANTS
VENDORS
DOCKERS
SAILORS
BEGGARS
COMMUTERS
GUARDS
CIVIL SERVANTS
PRESS
CIRCUS PERFORMERS
CREATURES
...and more!

Notes on Space

This play was written to commission from Regent's Park Open Air Theatre and as such was conceived to be somewhat site-specific. I encourage anyone staging this play elsewhere to take on the challenge of the play's scale as much as they dare, and to make any and all interventions they might need to in order to fit this beast into a new space. The point is to place the audience inside the action as it expands and to put them at the centre of a thriller!

Notes on Languages

The languages in the published text reflect the languages spoken by the company who first performed this play. Please feel free to adapt and add as many languages as you would care to in order to accurately reflect a diverse and bustling metropolis at the heart of a global empire.

Notes on Dance

This play opens and closes with a dance. I have made some suggestions in the stage directions where that dance might recur, but I am sure you will find more. Hopefully there is a way for you to thread your dance-language through your production of the piece. It might be a language that supports the storytelling and transitions but it will also be an opportunity for the play to speak without language to the world of the ensemble, who both support and conspire to revolt.

This text went to press before the end of previews and so may differ slightly from the play as performed.

Proem

Music! Our CHORUS *explode into a dance of frustration, fury and freedom. Among them, a lone figure (whom will we will refer to as 'TONGA' for now) dances his own dance. A dance of rage and rebellion and joy. These moves will echo throughout the piece and be reinvented at the end.*

Gradually the music of the dance is subsumed by gunfire, cannons, screaming and yelling. Suddenly, TONGA *is shackled and we realise we are in...*

Prologue

...India, 1857. SMALL, *a British soldier, sweaty, bloodied and panicking, crashes in. The sounds of a battle raging outside.*

SMALL. We've got a deal! We trade the treasure to get on the last boat out of here!

TONGA (*Hindustani*). *Kya tum unpar bharosa karte ho*? [Do you trust them?]

SMALL (*bad Hindustani*). 'Bharosa'? What's that? Trust?

TONGA (*Hindustani*). *Bharosa. Kya tum unpar bharosa karte ho*? [Trust. Do you trust them?]

SMALL. Trust Morstan and Sholto? No chance, mate. But the treasure – (*Bad Hindustani.*) *Khazana*, yeah, it'll buy us some trust.

TONGA. I give khazana *after* they give Padshah Begum Jahan.

SMALL. The Empress!? She's a political prisoner, mate, they're never gonna – No, her treasure is the only way we're getting out of here alive!

MORSTAN (*off*). Morstan, coming through!

SMALL *raises his gun as* MORSTAN*, confident and clean, enters, followed by* SHOLTO*, terrified.*

SMALL. STAND FAST!

MORSTAN. Private Small, we had an agreement.

SMALL (*lowering the rifle*). Just being careful, Captain Morstan.

MORSTAN. Well, there's nothing here except a man who should be behind bars, so –

SMALL. There will be, soon as you unshackle him.

SHOLTO. Don't, Morstan, it's some kind of trick –

SMALL. It's no trick, Mr Sholto. Was waiting for you, so's we'd all *trust* each other. Right?

TONGA (*indicating* MORSTAN *and* SHOLTO). Bharosa, no, bharosa them.

SHOLTO. What's he saying?

SMALL. He wants a deal. We know his Empress is on that boat.

MORSTAN. That is privileged / information.

SMALL. / So long as you get us aboard that ship and home with her, we'll give you a share.

SHOLTO. Of what? There's nothing here – / We need to leave.

SMALL. / Soon as we've got a deal, we'll get it for you.

MORSTAN. Enough. (*Leaving.*) Get him back in his cell and help to put down this mutiny.

SMALL. Your luck with the cards matches your luck with the colony girls, eh, Captain? We all know about your previous post –

MORSTAN. You dog!

SMALL. Could you live with *not* knowing how your luck might have changed if you'd just stuck around long enough to take a look?

An explosion, nearer this time.

SHOLTO. Captain Morstan, we don't have time / for this –

SMALL. / Won't be a Captain back home, just a man, full of debt with a little brown baby to explain to your wife.

MORSTAN *makes for* SMALL *but he raises his gun.*

We're this close to the Empress' treasure –

MORSTAN. Or to this slave making fools of us –

SMALL. Wouldn't take a minute to find out which.

After a moment's consideration, MORSTAN *relents and retrieves a key.*

MORSTAN. Be quick. (*Swapping the key for* SMALL*'s rifle.*) I'll keep the rifle on him.

SMALL *unlocks* TONGA*'s shackles as the fighting outside intensifies but* TONGA *doesn't move.*

SHOLTO. Captain, they're at the bloody walls.

SMALL. Mate. We've got no choice.

SHOLTO. What's he doing? Why isn't he getting it?

MORSTAN *cocks the rifle.*

SMALL. Get the treasure – *Khazana.* Get that bloody – (*Slapping* TONGA.) Now!

Reluctantly, TONGA *opens a secret compartment and draws out a bejewelled chest.*

MORSTAN. Well, I'll be…

SHOLTO. Bring it here, here!

SMALL. Good work, lad!! Going home now –

The sound of the encroaching battle grows as the men huddle for the chest, TONGA stops them.

TONGA (*Hindustani*). No. *Kasam. Jaan ki kasam. Yeh vada kabhi nahi tootega.* [Swear first. A blood oath. An unbreakable oath.]

SHOLTO. What's he saying? Why isn't he opening it?

SMALL. Cos he's right. We should swear first.

SMALL passes TONGA a knife – TONGA cuts his hand – and passes it to SMALL who follows suit.

On our blood. That this is ours, us four, as equals.

MORSTAN. Four?

SHOLTO. What use would it be to him?

SMALL. Swear.

SHOLTO. For Christ's sake! Fine, fine, just give me the… (*Cutting his hand.*) I swear. Morstan.

MORSTAN shoulders the rifle and takes the knife but hesitates.

SMALL. Oaths or nothing.

The battle-scape mutes to a pulse as MORSTAN cuts his hand. All four men hold their bleeding hands over the chest as TONGA and SMALL speak as if SMALL somehow is translating for TONGA.

TONGA. *Jo is pavitra vachan ko tode, us par laanat ho. Uski aakhri saans tak uska shikaar kiya jaye, uska peecha kiya jaye; aur shaitaan, bhoot aur zameen ki tamaam makhlooq uske peeche padi rahein, use jahannum tak ghaseet-te hue. Yeh khoon hum chaaron ki is kasam ko baandhta hai ke hum is khazane ko barabar baantenge.*

SMALL. / He who breaks this sacred vow be cursed. Hunted and dogged 'til his last breath, all the devils and demons and creatures of the earth be at their heels, chasing them to hell.

This blood so seals the solemn oath of we, the four, to share equally in this…

They open the box and are illuminated by the reflections of the treasures within. We see SHOLTO *and* MORSTAN *exchange a glance before* MORSTAN *shoots* SMALL *and then smashes* TONGA *with the butt, creating an explosion that reverberates and warps to become…*

ACT ONE

...a murmuring like rolling thunder beneath WATSON – alone, leaning on his stick and addressing us.

WATSON. London, 1890, the biggest city in the world at the height of the hottest summer ever recorded...

WATSON looks up at the weather, takes out his notepad, crosses something out and rewrites it.

WATSON. ...biggest city in the world at the (*Writing.*) *heart* of the sprawling British Empire.

With the word 'Empire', our CHORUS floods the stage.

WATSON. Having gained some notoriety in the renowned case *A Study in Scarlet*, Mr Sherlock Holmes is on the hunt for a new case!

SHERLOCK. Watson, I'd move if I were you.

SHERLOCK dings an invisible bell! The CHORUS become a raucous, sweaty crowd, gambling on SHERLOCK's boxing mis-match against ENZO 'BRICK JAW' GRAZIANO.

REFEREE. Gentlemen! You will fight to a finish. Time!

GRAZIANO descends on SHERLOCK and swiftly knocks him into the ropes. Cheers and groans from the crowd as money changes hands – WATSON swipes a paper in search of a different distraction.

GRAZIANO (*Italian*). *Chi altro*?! [Who's next?!]

WATSON. For God's sake, man, it's London! There has to be something better than this for you. Look, the Royal Engineers have lost a military air balloon.

SHERLOCK. Lost property? Seriously, Watson?! Come on, you big punchy bastard!

To everyone's surprise, SHERLOCK *launches at* GRAZIANO *and is – again – knocked down.*

WATSON goes to where SHERLOCK *is struggling to his feet*

WATSON. Here! 'Mystery body discovered behind locked doors.'

SHERLOCK (*spitting blood*). Mystery body discovered behind locked doors?

WATSON. 'A civil servant was found dead at Aldgate station – ' Holmes, a murder!

SHERLOCK. Too depressing. (*Back to the fight.*) RAGH!

Once more unto the boxing! SHERLOCK *manages to stay up slightly longer this time but is again knocked down –* WATSON *goes to him to use the news like a coach uses water.*

WATSON. 'Escape: Failures at London Zoo –' Animal breakouts, Holmes?!

SHERLOCK. Sounds like the plot of a children's book.

SHERLOCK *is struggling to his feet, clearly he should stay down.*

WATSON. Right – (*flipping some more.*) 'Obituary for ex-East India Company Governor, Sir Charles Sholto!'

SHERLOCK (*spitting blood*). No. Obituary means old news.

This time GRAZIANO *lands a vicious uppercut.*

GRAZIANO (*Italian*). *Avete visto*?! *Beccato da uno straniero!* [Did you see?! Caught by a foreigner!]

The REFEREE *declares* GRAZIANO *the winner – he celebrates.* SHERLOCK *slowly gets to his feet.*

WATSON. Ok. Well. This is the one for us, ready? Someone's lost their ticket to a show called 'The Wonders of the Empire'. Now, I know it's just a lost ticket but… What's all that?

SHERLOCK *is counting the notes he has stolen from* GRAZIANO.

SHERLOCK. Rent money.

WATSON. Did you just pick-pocket that!?

GRAZIANO *discovers his money to be gone and responds with fury.*

SHERLOCK. Don't see why he should get it when I'm the one doing all the hard work.

GRAZIANO (*Italian*). *Ladro*! [Thief!]

(*Strong Italian accent.*) Give me back my money!

GRAZIANO *descends on* SHERLOCK *but* WATSON *notices* MARY – *out of place in this shit-hole.*

WATSON. Holmes, you bloody idi – oh, hi.

MARY. Dr Watson?

WATSON. Hah. I mean, yes. I am… he.

MARY. Just as Mrs. Hudson described you.

WATSON. Is that a good thing or will I have to kill her? Hahaha… ahem.

MARY. She described a soldier. A doctor. Someone dedicated, through service, to his fellow man.

WATSON. That obvious, is it?

MARY. To those of us who care.

WATSON. Not many people do –

MARY. Oh, no, everyone knows, deep down at least, that the reason we're safe here is because of the sacrifices men like you have made far away. People like me really wouldn't be here without… Well, without you, really.

WATSON. Well, uh, that's – nice.

MARY (*retrieving a note*). Perhaps that's why, when I received this, it seemed only natural to turn to you and…

SHERLOCK *is getting pummelled.*

…is that Mr Holmes?

WATSON. Shall we find somewhere more fitting?

MARY. But you're at your leisure / and I'm interrupting.

WATSON. / Oh, no, I wouldn't normally come here – May I?

MARY (*handing over the note*). It arrived a few hours ago.

WATSON (*reading*). 'You have been wronged. Come alone, no police, to –' But this is urgent!

MARY. Yes, I came as soon as I could and… (*Retrieves a box.*) it arrived with this.

From the ropes, SHERLOCK *swipes the box.* GRAZIANO *is bearing down on him.*

SHERLOCK. Watson. The game is afoot!

SHERLOCK *spins and punches* GRAZIANO *who stumbles away as…*

…our CHORUS *conjure 221B Baker Street around* SHERLOCK. *He points* MARY *to the chair as he inspects the box.* WATSON *is pursuing him to try to stitch* SHERLOCK*'s lip.*

MARY. I've received a gift like this every year since my father's disappearance three years ago. Each sent with an incredible jewel and entirely anonymously, until tonight.

WATSON *starts stitching.*

WATSON. Don't talk.

SHERLOCK (*whilst* WATSON *holds his lip*). Yuh fa-ha – ?

WATSON. What did I just say?

MARY. Father? Captain Morstan, Indian regiment. Three years ago, he was here on leave for the first time in an age. He barely set foot in his own house before he was out of the door, no mention of where he was going… never to be seen again.

WATSON (*pausing his work*). I am so sorry. That's awful.

SHERLOCK (*lip still held*). Yeh, ruh-hish. Note?

SHERLOCK *exchanges the box for the note in* MARY*'s hand.*

MARY. There was an extensive police search but… nothing.

SHERLOCK. Nice! Likes his stationery almost as much you, Watso– (*His lip.*) – ow.

WATSON. I like other things as well – I don't mean – Sorry, that sounded – Anyway! Holmes, that should hold for now so long as you don't –

SHERLOCK. Cheltenham or Bath? It's the accent, much as you try to hide it, and, well, everything suggests an expensive boarding school.

MARY. Cheltenham.

SHERLOCK. Left-handed, sweaty. (*Reading.*) 'Be at the Lyceum Theatre at – (*Checking* WATSON*'s watch.*) Really bloody soon. (*Reading.*) 'Come alone, no police.' Your mother?

MARY. Oh, she died. A simple illness but –

SHERLOCK. – deadly in the colonies. So your mother – Sudanese? Egyptian! – threatened Captain Morstan with the scandal of his illegitimate daughter, namely you, and he paid her off with your education. You were not considered in the will and since he disappeared, likely dead, mysterious gifts – This is BRILLIANT! A secret guardian angel, Watson! A chance to see if there really ever is anything more than basic animal greed in this seething cess pit… what?

WATSON. Holmes.

WATSON *is indicating* MARY *who is visibly upset.*

SHERLOCK.…there's a little leftover opium in the pipe. I'll start it off for you, just… knock out a few earwigs… this thing is *infested* with them.

WATSON *snatches the packet of matches from* SHERLOCK. SHERLOCK *persists with the pipe.*

WATSON. We may not be inspiring much confidence but one thing we certainly are… is not the police.

WATSON *snatches the pipe from* SHERLOCK*'s mouth.*

If you'll have us, it would be our pleasure to accompany you.

MARY. But Mr Holmes' eye –

SHERLOCK. It's fine, Miss…?

MARY. Call me Mary.

MRS HUDSON *enters, carrying a red envelope.*

MRS HUDSON. Final Warning on the rent, SherlohmyGOD! A visitor!

WATSON. We're actually working.

MRS HUDSON. You boys have never had a lady over before. Sherlock's more of an Oscar Wilde type.

SHERLOCK. Who?

MRS HUDSON. And this one's never had any guests at all.

WATSON. I wouldn't say 'never' –

MRS HUDSON. Cup of tea, love?

WATSON. We're actually on a case so if you could / call us a cab.

MRS HUDSON. / It's a brew, calm down – (*To* SHERLOCK.) You. This. Important.

SHERLOCK *takes the red envelope and pockets it for much, much later.*

SHERLOCK. I'll treasure it.

MRS HUDSON. Christ alive! What happened to his face?

SHERLOCK. I was practising –

MRS HUDSON. What, getting beaten up? (*Spitting on a handkerchief.*) C'mere.

WATSON. Mrs Hudson, / we're working –

SHERLOCK. / No! TAXI!!

A cab forms around SHERLOCK, WATSON *and* MARY. SHERLOCK*'s lip is bleeding.*

DRIVER. Lyceum Theatre, mate?

WATSON (*helping* MARY *aboard*). On the double.

SHERLOCK. If you've received three gifts such as this, why still work as a governess?

MARY. How did you know?

SHERLOCK. Milk stain on your sleeve, pocket bible, faint grass stain around the height of a child's foot when carried –

WATSON (*making notes*). Slow down, slow down.

SHERLOCK. Watson wants you to notice that he's writing a book.

MARY. Another one!? Fabulous!

WATSON. You know about the first – ?

MARY. *A Study in Scarlet*? Loved it! How else do you imagine I'd heard of you?

SHERLOCK. Do you often take professional recommendations from the fiction section?

MARY. When desperate, Mr Holmes, a woman goes on faith.

SHERLOCK. Who did your father know in London?

MARY. No one really. Almost his entire life was spent abroad. The only non-military people he knew would have worked for the East India Company –

SHERLOCK. Like the one who died recently of a heart attack.

VENDOR (*outside*). Sir Charles Sholto, dead of heart attack.

SHERLOCK. We're here.

SHERLOCK *hops out of the cab and our* CHORUS *become a crowd of Londoners outside the Lyceum. Among them, flashes of colour; lizards, parakeets.* SHERLOCK *takes a newspaper from* VENDOR *and, as* SHERLOCK *expected,* WATSON *pays whilst* MARY *is gripped under the arm by* WILLIAMS.

WILLIAMS. He told you, come alone.

WATSON. Oi, let go of her or –

WILLIAMS. Or what?

WATSON. She is under my protection –

SHERLOCK. I wouldn't, Watson. Williams here knocked me out in two rounds last weekend.

WILLIAMS (*shaking hands*). Mr Holmes! Didn't recognise you with the tenderloin.

SHERLOCK. We couldn't let the lady come alone, could we?

WILLIAMS. Course, mate. This way.

WILLIAMS *leads them through London and somewhere, an animal rumbles and snorts loudly.*

MARY. What's that!?

WATSON. Another zoo escapee, I expect.

WILLIAMS. Bloody nuisance. You gonna eat that?

SHERLOCK *hands over the steak and* WILLIAMS *eats it as they set off.*

MARY. If they've escaped, why on Earth don't they head directly home? What good do these animals do us by simply hanging around?

(*To Watson.*) You've improved their home countries tenfold, there's no space here for such savage beasts – London is full!

Something scampers by, making MARY *cling to* WATSON.

WATSON. You're safe with us, Mary. I'm a military man.

SHERLOCK (*his head in his paper*). And only a little damaged.

WATSON. My knee. Afghanistan.

SHERLOCK. Sometimes it's his shoulder – He doesn't need the stick.

MARY. In my experience, pain, like grief, follows its own logic, a logic that can't be understood by those who cause it. It's incredible that you managed to write such an intelligent book whilst suffering so.

WATSON. I was really just attempting to illuminate Mr Holmes' techniques –

SHERLOCK. He didn't.

WATSON. Well, I've taken *some* artistic licence, but Mr Holmes' science of deduction is –

SHERLOCK. Rendered a complete fantasy.

WATSON. Haha – he didn't read it – You didn't even read it!

SHERLOCK. People read that book the way a drowning man clings to a log. Desperate for the illusion of order in this miasma of greed and self-service.

SHERLOCK *hops into a second taxi, followed by* WATSON *and* MARY. WILLIAMS *is too focussed on his steak to notice.*

This way! I know where we're going.

MARY. Really? How – ?

SHERLOCK (*to* WILLIAMS). Thank you, Williams, we know the way from here.

WILLIAMS. What – ? Oi!

WATSON *and* MARY *jump aboard just as the taxi begins to move.*

WATSON. Ah, Tower Bridge! The world's first combination of a / bascule and suspension…

MARY. / Bascule and suspension bridge. The steam-power should mean it can open in / about a minute.

WATSON. / About a minute. Did you hear, a snake infestation forced construction / to a halt?

MARY. / To a halt! Yes! London does keep growing, doesn't it?

WATSON. I expect you've kept up with the state of the art prison at Wormwood? The embankments, Smithfield's – It really is the most sophisticated city in the world.

SHERLOCK. Not sophisticated, Watson, she said 'growing' Like a tumour. And in case anyone cares – (*Chucking his paper out of the window.*) we are on our way to Pondicherry Lodge.

DRIVER. Oh, a well-known residence –

SHERLOCK. – belonging to the late Sir Charles Sholto.

MARY. But how can you possibly know?

WATSON (*ready to take notes*). Here we go.

SHERLOCK. These gifts began to arrive *after* Captain Morstan's disappearance. You came to us shortly *after* the death of one of the few men he would have known. Sir Charles Sholto. He sent you those first two boxes from a sense of what? Guilt? And now, *after* his death, you receive a third box but with a hurried note describing you as 'wronged' and requesting a clandestine meeting. The author must be close enough to Sholto to have access to his wealth and to keep his secrets, therefore it could only possibly be –

MARY. His son and heir!

WATSON (*looking up from his frantic scribbling*). What, really?

MARY. Those books of yours must be working *after* all, Doctor!

SHERLOCK (*annoyed*). Mr Thaddeus Sholto.

WATSON *helps* MARY *from the cab and into…*

...Pondicherry Lodge. THADDEUS *is stood in a
resplendent and wealthy room full of curiosities from the
far-flung corners of the British Empire and servants in
exoticised uniforms. Among them, a kukri, a Nepalese
curved knife.*

THADDEUS. The wronged woman! Thank goodness you're
here but –

MARY. Allow me to introduce my friend Dr Watson / and his –

THADDEUS. / I expressly forbad – They must leave! / Now,
please –

SHERLOCK. / You couldn't expect her to come *alone*,
Thaddeus? May I call you Thaddeus?

THADDEUS. No, you may not, sir –

MARY. This is the soon-to-be renowned detective, Sherlock
Holmes –

THADDEUS. Police!?

SHERLOCK. No, more of a hobby.

THADDEUS. Madam, this – this changes things, I intended for
a private discussion to resolve –

SHERLOCK. – Why so private?

THADDEUS. – some sensitive – Because it regards
something –

SHERLOCK. Incriminating?

THADDEUS. Will you please!?

SHERLOCK. Why all the secrecy and prize-fighters?

THADDEUS. Because Papa was claimed by The Curse!

SHERLOCK. Not a heart attack then.

THADDEUS. No! What sort of heart attack leaves a man with
a – a horrible smiling – face? And before you say it, no, it
couldn't have been rigor mortis, I was here moments *after* –

After whatever was done to him. The investigation has been far from – Moreover, I summoned this lady here to do her justice.

SHERLOCK. How has she been wronged, Thaddeus?

THADDEUS. Papa… You have to understand that India, it… it changed him. He returned pursued by a shadow. Plagued by waking nightmares, muttering about being hunted, paranoid and – his world shrank first to the size of London, then of this house, then this room. He never left but once –

SHERLOCK. Three years ago.

MARY. But that was when my father –

SHERLOCK. – disappeared, yes. You know hat happened to Captain Morstan?

THADDEUS. Papa told me – Well, as I've said, he wasn't a well man –

SHERLOCK. His exact words, please.

SHOLTO *enters.* SHERLOCK, WATSON *and* MARY *are in the presence of a ghost.*

SHOLTO. I have a weight upon me… A curse. Lurking in the half-light, waiting – That jewel, beside the kukri, the knife. It is part, a small part of much, much more.

SHERLOCK. More what?

SHOLTO. Treasure, boy. Cursed treasure. Morstan and I, we liberated it during the Indian Mutiny. Tonight, he came to claim his share.

SHERLOCK. But the Mutiny was thirty years prior and you say this was the first time Morstan had been back in all that time?

THADDEUS. It was the soonest he was permitted leave to return –

WATSON. Refused leave for *thirty years*?

SHERLOCK. Sholto would have known Morstan's superiors from his time at the East India Company, correct?

THADDEUS. Oh, yes, Papa was great friends with generals and admirals –

SHERLOCK. Whom he bribed to keep Morstan away from home and the treasure.

SHOLTO. Listen to me! The treasure… Only Morstan's illegitimate child can slake its thirst for blood – She has been wronged. The treasure must go to her, piece by piece, year on –

SHERLOCK. No. There's something missing –

THADDEUS. But this is precisely why I summoned the lady –

SHERLOCK. Morstan had staked his claim earlier that night, he barely set foot in his own house before he was here.

MORSTAN (*older*) *enters and silently addresses* SHOLTO *– who commentates on what we see, whilst fetching* MORSTAN *a drink and interacting.*

SHOLTO. Finally, *after* all this time as I knew he would be, but so full of the colonies, all rage and revenge. Demanding half when he was due a quarter, we'd sworn a blood oath to it. He sprang from his chair, stumbled and… was dead.

SHERLOCK. He… fell?

MORSTAN *springs from his chair, stumbles and drops dead.*

THADDEUS. And hit his head, incredibly unlucky –

WATSON. Oh, Mary, my deepest sympathies –

SHERLOCK (*to* MARY). Me too – (*To* THADDEUS.) You're sure those were his exact words?

WATSON. Gentlemen, please. Have a care.

THADDEUS. Ah, yes, I am afraid, Madam, that we are both orphans and in that sense, related. A drink? Yes? Chai, perhaps?

SHERLOCK. He specifically mentioned the jewel and this knife to you?

THADDEUS. Look, none of this is relevant to the – the gifts Papa sent to this lady every year –

SHERLOCK. Why the change of heart? He'd sat with this treasure for decades, why then?

SHERLOCK lifts the kukri – as he does so, so too does MORSTAN lift back to his feet. Replaying his previous silent scene with SHOLTO from just before the argument.

THADDEUS. Because he, only he, recognised she had been wronged! He did so from a sense of –

This time, when MORSTAN springs to his feet it is to take the drink offered by SHOLTO in the cup...

SHERLOCK. Guilt. His exact words, Thaddeus, you owe her this.

SHOLTO. He sprang from his chair and...

SHOLTO takes the kukri from SHERLOCK and slams it into MORSTAN – MARY yelps.

No one knew he had ever been here... Why should anyone ever know?

THADDEUS takes the knife from SHOLTO, cleans and replaces it where it was displayed.

THADDEUS. I told you India had changed him.

SHERLOCK. The body. His first words to you were about a weight. 'I have a weight upon me.'

SHOLTO wraps MORSTAN's body in the rug on which he fell and starts to heave it off.

THADDEUS. Yes. The last time Papa left this room, the only time in years...

THADDEUS helps SHOLTO drag MORSTAN's body off.

SHERLOCK. Was when you helped him to sink Morstan's body in the Thames.

MARY. Is that… true? *(Retrieving her Bible.)* Oh, good God.

WATSON. You've known for *three years*!

THADDEUS. Three *terrible* years of holding that secret, watching his decline – Until but days ago The Curse that dogged Papa finally found him – Here, in this very chair. We must right their wrongs – Madam, Papa was gifting you the treasure piecemeal that it might not arouse suspicion – Madam, it should be ours. You and I can liberate that treasure once more and lift The Curse!

SHERLOCK. You don't know where it is.

THADDEUS. No, it's – It's here. Somewhere. We've searched the grounds, emptied every openable thing – Even dug the cellar. It's waiting for us to – to share, Madam!

SHERLOCK. You thought she might know, that your father might have given her a clue of some kind, didn't you?

THADDEUS. He had always protected me from it.

SHERLOCK *(to* MARY*)*. Do you have the box?

MARY *(passing it)*. Here. I want no part of that blood-money –

THADDEUS. But this – It's the wealth of the Mughal dynasty! It once belonged to their last living heir – An Empress!

WATSON. The lady has spoken, Thaddeus. Send for the police.

Someone leaves to fetch (become) the police. WATSON *retrains* THADDEUS *with cuffs? A rope?*

THADDEUS. Police!? No, you can't –

WATSON. You are an accomplice to a murder!

THADDEUS. There's no need for – I was only interested in the lady's well-being and – and lifting this terrible –

SHERLOCK. Curse, yes. Let's make sure it isn't *all* make believe, shall we? Your father implied it was all held in one place, if it were a chest the contents to date infer a certain size. Considering Sholto barricaded himself in here, it makes sense he'd do so with his precious treasure in sight. The height of the ceiling… suggests the walls or floor… A small symbol on the box, matching this –

SHERLOCK *moves something that looks like it shouldn't move and unlocks…*

WATSON (*starting to make notes*). Incredible.

…a secret hatch to reveal – the treasure from the prologue!

THADDEUS. My goodness!! My goodness!

MARY *swoons,* WATSON *catches her. Her Bible falls to the floor.*

WATSON. She needs some air. Holmes! The window!

SHERLOCK *opens the window.*

MARY. Can't breathe –

WATSON. Outside. Holmes, the door!

SHERLOCK. Thaddeus, the authorities will be with you shortly.

THADDEUS. A jury will acquit me!

SHERLOCK. Thank you for the case.

As WATSON *and* SHERLOCK *help* MARY, *our* CHORUS *creates the space outside the front door:*

MARY (*bursting out*). I'm sorry – I just – I couldn't be in that place any more.

WATSON. Perfectly understandable, Mary –

SHERLOCK. Yes, you've finally learned that your father was violently murdered and the gifts were from his killer.

WATSON. My apologies, Mary.

SHERLOCK. Well, none of us seriously suspected altruism, did we? Doesn't exist! And we've all been so focussed on your dead father, we've not yet asked the real question: Who killed Sir Charles Sholto?

WATSON. Mr Holmes has spent so long numbing himself with violence and drugs that he's almost forgotten he has a human heart –

SHERLOCK. The heart is a muscle and you're obsessed with the drugs! They're chemicals, all we are – All of this is chemical, Watson. The drugs help me see things, connections, the bigger picture –

WATSON. Helped you see a dog-sized rat behind our wallpaper –

SHERLOCK. I shot it, didn't I?

WATSON. It was a hallucination! And guess who's still paying off the neighbours?

MARY. Excuse me. I… I left my bible.

WATSON. Of course, Mary. Would you like me to – ?

MARY. Thank you, I'll be fine.

MARY *returns towards the house.* WATSON *and* SHERLOCK *conduct an initially hushed conversation:*

SHERLOCK. Really?

WATSON. What?

SHERLOCK. You barely know her.

WATSON. Feelings aren't based on research, Holmes. Besides, she's above my station.

SHERLOCK. She's a governess.

WATSON. Not once she's received half of that treasure. Besides, right now, she is a woman in need.

SHERLOCK. Exactly, it's disgusting.

WATSON. This is the altruism you've been looking for and you call it 'disgusting' –

SHERLOCK. Altruism – You want her. If that's not naked greed then it's personal gain.

WATSON. Holmes. If you had to choose between a situation where you win, but lose a loved one –

SHERLOCK. Hypotheticals, Watson.

WATSON. Or lose but save the loved one –

SHERLOCK. What would I be winning?

WATSON. Dunno, cleverest man award – The fact you're even asking –

SHERLOCK. Personal gain, Watson. It's the only order there is to all this.

WATSON. God you're depressing.

SHERLOCK. The lie is depressing – You know better and yet you're willing to suspend your own intelligence for… Her.

WATSON. Are you jealous?

SHERLOCK. Course I'm not jealous! That'd require –

WATSON. A heart that's more than a muscle?

INSEPCTOR LESTRADE *and a* POLICE OFFICER *arrive.*

LESTRADE. Allo, allo, allo! If it isn't Tweedledum and Tweedle-dickhead.

SHERLOCK. I thought they sent for the authorities –

LESTRADE. Funny little joke that, cos we actually are the authorities, and armchair vigilantes are the last thing we need, what with the psycho in Whitechapel and rhinos in the parks. Eff off and come up with another kids' story for that rag.

WATSON. Beeton's Christmas Annual is a respected literary –

LESTRADE. And 'Eff off' is a respected stand in for 'Fuck off'. Come on, let's see if we can't confiscate some jewels.

A scream from off.

WATSON. Mary!

SHERLOCK *and* WATSON *run, pursued by* LESTRADE *and* POLICE OFFICER*, back into…*

…Pondicherry Lodge, where THADDEUS *is dead in the chair he had been restrained to. His face contorted into a smiling grimace. The key and the treasure gone.* MARY *clutching her Bible, staring.*

Mary? Are you okay?

LESTRADE. Hullo. Is his face normally like that?

SHERLOCK (*checking* THADDEUS *'pulse*). He's dead. And the treasure's gone.

MARY. The Curse.

POLICE. *Déjà vu*, innit? We was here for his old man not a week ago –

SHERLOCK. Same muscle tension? Smiling face?

POLICE OFFICER *nods and* SHERLOCK *begins to investigate the room as* LESTRADE *makes his own deductions.*

LESTRADE. Is this the fella we're here to arrest? Hang about… How long was she alone with him?

WATSON. Lestrade, I know you're overstretched but really?

MARY. It's The Curse.

LESTRADE. She would've had to share the rich stuff with him, eh?

WATSON. You can't seriously be accusing Mary –

LESTRADE. Suspecting, Doctor, it's a technical term. Why's this tea smell funny, love?

SHERLOCK. Wasn't the chai, for poison to work this quickly, she would have had to introduce it directly into the blood. She had the obvious motive and opportunity, of course, but –

WATSON. Holmes!?

SHERLOCK. Watson, he's like a pitbull with a child's leg.

LESTRADE. Determined's the word you're looking for. This way, Ma'am

MARY. I'd like a moment to pray for him, if I may –

LESTRADE. Would you, love? No you mayn't. (*To* POLICE.) Cuff her. Arresting you on suspicion of murder.

WATSON. Lestrade, this is ridiculous!

LESTRADE. You'll want to get word to your family.

MARY. But I don't – Dr Watson, I don't have anyone!

WATSON. You have me. Lestrade, if you'll just allow her to tell you what / happened.

LESTRADE. / Course, yeah, down at the station. / Come on now.

LESTRADE *leads* MARY *away, whilst* POLICE OFFICER *holds* WATSON *back.*

WATSON. / For God's sake, Mary, we'll prove this wasn't you. I give you my word!

SHERLOCK. Romantic promise, Watson. How are you gonna deliver on it?

WATSON. She's innocent, Holmes – Her motive, the treasure, it's gone –

SHERLOCK. This is what it all comes down to, Watson. Rats in a cage fighting over the last scraps of a world that is slowly turning back to dust.

WATSON. You said Sholto's killer was still at large. Well, it's either The Curse or an impossible murder.

SHERLOCK. It is a good game, I'll give you that.

WATSON. Mary's life depends on us – Solve this, Sherlock. It may be a game to you; it isn't to me.

SHERLOCK. To you it's an evolutionary drive that's become a delusion –

WATSON. Please, Sherlock. *Beat.*

SHERLOCK. Don't touch him! What kind of a poison are we looking at?

The POLICE OFFICER *who was about to move* SHOLTO*'s body stands back as* SHERLOCK *begins his examination.*

WATSON. Something fast, Curare perhaps? Strychnine? But as you said, it'd have to be introduced directly into the… (SHERLOCK *is holding a thorn.*) Was that in his ear?

Using a hankie, WATSON *carefully takes the thorn from* SHERLOCK.

SHERLOCK. He must have been looking at the treasure. Which is why he didn't notice the blowgun. Recognise it?

WATSON. It's a thorn, not native. Saw something similar in – Sorry, *blowgun*?

SHERLOCK. The window.

WATSON *leaves his stick behind as they go to the window.*

WATSON. But it's a sheer drop –

SHERLOCK. – unless the assassin had… Here!

SHERLOCK *and* WATSON *climb onto the window ledge. A well-tied rope hangs from here down to the ground outside.* SHERLOCK *inspects the knot.*

Possibly a sailor. (*On the rope.*) Blood. Suggests he's lost the hands for it.

WATSON. He can't have gone far –

SHERLOCK *grabs onto the rope and, as he lowers himself down, everything changes…*

…SHERLOCK *lands on the street outside Pondicherry Lodge.* WATSON *joins but has left his stick.*

SHERLOCK. Mind your step, the data's here somewhere.

WATSON. Footprints? Holmes, it's Brixton Market.

All of London life is here; VENDORS, LABOURERS, BEGGARS, SAILORS *and all of it is trampling the data.*

SHERLOCK. He had to have passed this way.

WATSON (*drawing his revolver*). What if he hasn't gone? What if he's keeping watch? Covering his escape?

SHERLOCK. Put it away, he wouldn't waste a head start by hanging around.

WATSON. We don't know how he thinks, that's what went wrong in Afghanistan.

SHERLOCK. Uneven prints, here, all around.

WATSON. We thought we were hunting them, they were hunting us all along.

SHERLOCK. Our man has trouble walking. But climbing, firing, retrieving the chest…

WATSON. Must be a monster. We'll need to be on our guard…

SHERLOCK closes his eyes, WATSON*'s voice and the sounds of London muffle and distort – we hear* SHOLTO*'s muffled voice replaying in* SHERLOCK*' mind.*

SHOLTO. …all rage and revenge. Demanding half when he was due a quarter, we'd sworn a blood oath to it.

WATSON (*snapping* SHERLOCK *out of it*). SHERLOCK! He's getting away –

SHERLOCK. 'They', Watson. They! Four people stole that treasure from India. Morstan and Sholto are dead, we're *after* the remaining two.

WATSON. Okay, great. Which way did they go?

SHERLOCK. They knew the treasure had to be in that room but *after* they killed Sholto, there was no time, they couldn't find it. They stayed nearby, kept watch, until Thaddeus was alone and… I showed them where it was hidden.

WATSON. Just now? You mean they were watching – They saw that!?

SHERLOCK (*picking up a cigarette butt*). One man, about six-feet tall, ex-sailor who suffered some kind of leg injury that still affects his walk. He waited here, smoking, whilst…

We see a man matching this description – SMALL – at the base of the rope.

The second climbed, aimed… and went in for the treasure.

We see TONGA at the top of the rope doing just that before disappearing from view.

WATSON (*finishing some notes*). Fantastic… Now where are they?

SHERLOCK. I'm working on it –

WATSON. We need a dog! That mongrel, what's its name, Keith or – ?

SHERLOCK. The chest! Too obvious and heavy to carry.

TONGA *drops the chest from the top of the rope into a waiting cart, loaded with sacks of coffee beans to cushion the landing. Beans explode from the back. SHERLOCK picks one up.*

…coffee beans. A barrow.

WATSON. Wheel prints – This way… Wait, they've been… Gah, it's hopeless!

SHERLOCK. They can't sell it in England without drawing scrutiny, they'll need to get it out of the country and quickly – They'll leave by the best means they know.

WATSON. Sailors – The docks! But the river's covered in them…

SHERLOCK *is licking another cigarette butt.*

Oh, great.

SHERLOCK. Cigarettes Laurens. I knew a man who used to smoke these, French Navy, you can't get them in London.

WATSON. Holmes, every minute we waste is another Lestrade can spend trying to pin all of this on Mary. We have to retrieve her rightful inheritance!

SHERLOCK *is finding connections on the floor – broken-up tracks, prints, and spilled coffee beans.*

SHERLOCK. She has no 'rightful inheritance', she's illegitimate.

WATSON. Compensation, then.

SHERLOCK. And we should compensate people based on who they're related to?

WATSON. For what her father clearly did to her mother.

SHERLOCK. What about what was done to the entire population for whom those heirlooms are worth more than just money? That treasure isn't free wealth, Watson, it's stolen history and I've no idea where they went from here.

WATSON, *who has been hobbling all this time, spots a beggar – later we will know him as* DOMINGO.

WATSON. You! We're looking for two sailors pulling a coffee cart, one smoking, limping – ?

DOMINGO *holds out a hand.*

(*Searching out a coin.*) Beginning to think Holmes is right about personal gain –

DOMINGO *takes the coin and points.*

WATSON. Thank you – Holmes! (WATSON *leads.*) They can keep the bloody treasure so long as we prove Mary's innocence.

SHERLOCK. I think it's important, both for you and for your future readers, that you start to see – No, accept that we're doing this for you, not Mary.

WATSON. Hey, I'm not going pretend this won't make a brilliant book. But only if we nail the ending and we won't do that if Mary's… that's still lit…

SHERLOCK *has picked up a smouldering cigarette butt.*

SHERLOCK. They're nearby.

WATSON. Stay behind me, Holmes, you're the one who – Oi!

A sign reading 'Smith's Boat Hire: By Hour or Day'.
SHERLOCK *punches* WATSON*'s hat. The London that*
surrounds them now is a dock; IMMIGRANT WORKERS,
varied cargo, SEX WORKERS.

That's my best hat.

SHERLOCK. Turn your coat inside out. If they recognise us,
we'll lose them.

WATSON. Where's my stick?

SHERLOCK. Don't let on – (*Becoming a character.*) Hullo,
Ma'am! Gaffer about?

ALEKSANDRA. Ooh, you only just missed 'im. Couple o'
passengers in a rush.

SHERLOCK. Posh types, eh?

ALEKSANDRA. Colony types. Tryna get out to the bigger
boats and away to God knows where. Truth be told, the tall
one put me in mind of them Whitechapel murders. More
animal than man. 'Ere 'bout a boat?

SHERLOCK. Your steam launch, heard she's a belter.

ALEKSANDRA. Fastest on the river. But that's the one they
took.

WATSON. Where were they headed – ?

SHERLOCK. Ah, that's a shame. Back soon or – ?

ALEKSANDRA. Ain't got the coals to take her further than
Rotherhithe, 'specially 'gainst the tide. They'll be back
tomorrow.

SHERLOCK. No chance they'll buy coal down river? Keep
goin'?

ALEKSANDRA. Not likely, prices they charge and working an engine in this heat. They'll be waiting out the tide somewhere down river now.

SHERLOCK (*to* WATSON). Waiting out the tide somewhere east of here but not further than Rotherhithe.

WATSON. We should go –

ALEKSANDRA. Right-ho. Nothing else I can give you? Set on the steamer they took?

SHERLOCK. If it's the one I heard about, what's it called now?

ALEKSANDRA. *The Aurora.*

SHERLOCK. Yeah, green, yellow line, broad in the beam?

ALEKSANDRA. *Aurora*'s a trim little thing. Fresh painted, black with two red streaks. It's *Damsel* you're thinking of, she's free if you've – ?

SHERLOCK. Nah, we'll wait. Black funnel, weren't it?

ALEKSANDRA. With a white band.

SHERLOCK. That's it. We'll check back tomorrow. Ta, love.

WATSON. What's the second-fastest boat you have?

SHERLOCK. Come on, mate –

WATSON. But Holmes –

SHERLOCK. Who? (*Leading him away in a headlock.*) Get a coupla drinks in ya, and you're mad –

The dock swarms around SHERLOCK *and* WATSON *as our* CHORUS *gradually creates…*

WATSON. Off me! (*Struggling free.*)

SHERLOCK. Are you trying to warn them they're being followed?

WATSON. But they're gonna switch to a bigger boat and away to the colonies!

SHERLOCK. Not until the tide changes. For now, they're stuck.

WATSON. Then we should get ahead of them!

SHERLOCK. How?

WATSON. I dunno, you're the genius!

SHERLOCK. Our only chance is to get eyes all over the river so the moment *The Aurora* breaks cover, we can get *after* her on the fastest boat we can find. We'll need help.

WATSON. Great, about time we sent for the police –

SHERLOCK. Watson, I said *help*.

...a rough and bustling pub. LUCIA *working the bar.*

(*To* LUCIA.) A pint each, cheers, Lucia.

WATSON. Daytime pints? Holmes, Mary's in a cell –

POCKETS. This is everyone for the moment, sir.

No sooner has LUCIA *placed a crowd of pints down than they're snaffled by a dozen hands. The pub is full of* UNEMPLOYED DOCKERS, EX-SAILORS *and* BEGGARS – *all quaffing their pints.*

SHERLOCK. I need word on a steamer named *Aurora*, black, white stripe on the funnel, two red on the hull.

SLY SYD. *Aurora*'s the fastest on the river.

SHERLOCK. Then I need to know the moment she hits the Thames. She's moored somewhere between here and Rotherhithe.

POCKETS. We can run word down Rotherhithe but...

JEAN (*French*). *Il n'y a pas moyen que j'y aille là bas. Peu importe combien il paie.* [There's no way I'm going there, not matter how much he pays.]

SHERLOCK. What's that?

POCKETS. There's rumours about summat around the Salt Quays.

TOMMO. A creature, they say sings instead of speaks –

SLY SYD. Nah, that one's in Hyde Park.

POCKETS. They say there's things in all the parks at night.

SHERLOCK. I don't want rumours, I want that boat. And this man will pay good money to whoever spots her first.

All but one of the BAKER STREET IRREGULARS *finish their drinks and leave.*

WATSON. Holmes, some of them weren't more than children.

SHERLOCK. Scotland Yard has its regulars, Baker Street has its irregulars.

WATSON. Is that meant to be a joke?

SHERLOCK. Noticed you didn't write it down.

WATSON. These people are addicts, they need help not –

SHERLOCK. It's paid work, they're good at it. Nothing more invisible in this town than the poor.

WATSON. But you know what they'll spend the money on. At least offer them food instead, that'd be –

SHERLOCK. Better for your conscience? Let them escape for God's sake –

WATSON. They're sick, Sherlock!

SHERLOCK. They're casualties. (*Downs a pint.*) You know the worst slave owners are the ones who are *nice* to their slaves.

WATSON. What on earth has slavery got to do / with this?

SHERLOCK. / False charity. All of this is built on their blood. Your blood. It's all unethical, stop pretending otherwise and stop hobbling, it's all in your head.

WATSON. Serving one's country is not unethical. And I didn't get shot in my head.

SHERLOCK. I thought you were serving Afghans? Or is that just what they told the rest of us?

WATSON. I think you need a rest.

SHERLOCK (*leaving*). I think you're right.

WATSON. I'll find us a boat, then. I mean *actual* rest, Holmes!

LUCIA. Two pound six.

> SHERLOCK *has gone and* WATSON *is confused.*

For the pints. Two pound six.

WATSON. Bloody hell. Does that include service? Robbery. (*Paying.*) I want change for that.

LUCIA (*Portuguese*). *Filho da puta.* [Son of a bitch.]

WATSON. Excuse me?

> SLIP JENNY *crashes in.*

SLIP JENNY. Mr Holmes?! They've sped up her case – Where's the sad, lonely fella with the pints?

WATSON. Whose case? Look, he's gone, just –

SLIP JENNY. The Sholto murderess!

WATSON. Mary?

SLIP JENNY. He had me watching the courthouse –

WATSON. Take me there! Now!

> LUCIA *is left to pocket the change as London swirls to reveal…*

> *…a* JUDGE *in a courthouse and* MARY *in the dock.*

JUDGE. Madam. You have repaid England's hospitality poorly indeed. And though your late father *tried* to civilise you, your heinous actions against two valued members of this society demonstrate a / failure to better…

MARY. / Your honour, at least allow me to offer some defence –

JUDGE. As I was saying! You have failed to better your savage nature and have been found GUILTY of murder and shall be sentenced tomorrow!

MARY. No! No, please!

WATSON. Mary! Mary, we'll find who really did this.

Commotion as MARY is pulled away by POLICE, WATSON in pursuit. PRESS and PUBLIC chatter and hurl abuse. One figure in the crowd is dancing a dance reminiscent of the prologue.

POLICE. / Sir! If you could!

WATSON. Don't give up hope. This isn't – / It's not right!

MARY. / Dr Watson! They wouldn't even let me take my bible –

WATSON. For God's sake, man! Show a little humanity!

WATSON stomps over to where LESTRADE is holding her Bible, grabs it from him and hands it to her.

LESTRADE. Alright, mate –

WATSON. We'll find them, Mary – We'll prove you're innocent!

LESTRADE. You can always enjoy a romantic visit down Wormwood Scrubs.

As MARY is taken away, smoke swirls, and now the COURTHOUSE CROWD all seem to be slow-dancing and collapsing as we enter…

WATSON (*searching*). Holmes!?

…the Jade Dragon, an opium den in Limehouse. LIN and BILL are sharing a cigarette.

LIN. And I said, 'Mate, that's not a horse, it's a giraffe, it shouldn't even be – '

WATSON. I'm looking for Mr Sherlock Holmes, he's a regular here.

LIN (*Mandarin*). 客官貴安, 裡面請 [*Kè guān guì ān, lǐ miàn qǐng.*] [Good evening, Sir. Welcome.]

WATSON (*spelling it out*). Yes, I am looking. For. Someone. Here –

LIN (*in character*). This is a place of peace, sir. Please, leave your troubles –

WATSON. No, I don't want any of this poison and, frankly –

LIN (*dropping character*). Bloody trouble-makers. Bill! Get rid of him!

BILL *emerges, cracking his knuckles.*

WATSON. No, I'm looking for a friend –

A pile of clothes raises a hand, it's SHERLOCK *and he's all kinds of messed up.*

SHERLOCK. Watson. Is the boat awake yet?

WATSON (*trying to lift him*). Holmes, Mary's life is in our hands.

SHERLOCK. Is this ink? You're a pencils man. You signed in somewhere.

WATSON. Come on. Get up!

SHERLOCK. You're the one lying on the ceiling. This odd clay on your boot, it's only found at the courthouse!

WATSON. They're pinning both Sholto murders on Mary! I need something to wake him up. The strongest you have.

LIN. Mr Sherlock gave that stuff up.

WATSON (*forking out*). Here.

BILL *takes the money and nods for* LIN *to fetch a syringe.*

BILL (*counting the money*). You should know, mate. Market's flooded with cheap opium, which means the stuff you're *after* –

WATSON (*lifting* SHERLOCK *again*). Let me guess, it's expensive? Can you stand?

SHERLOCK (*collapsing*). Yep.

WATSON (*trying and failing to lift him*). SHERLOCK! Mary needs us!

LIN *returns,* WATSON *snatches the syringe from her and rolls up* SHERLOCK*'s sleeve.*

SHERLOCK. Wait, what are you doing? No. No, I stopped with that – Lin, tell him I stopped –

WATSON. Her life is in our hands.

SHERLOCK. But John… The hypothetical… Between saving someone or winning something – ?

WATSON. I choose saving the loved one.

WATSON *injects* SHERLOCK *with cocaine. Everything warps and changes as our* CHORUS *takes us to…*

…the incredibly incongruous atmosphere of The Diogenes Club. Suits, top hats, silverware against porcelain, a clock ticking and the rustling of newspapers. But then SHERLOCK *bursts in:*

SHERLOCK. MYCROFT! I'll do you a deal!

He is followed by WATSON *who is engaged in a physical struggle with two* SECURITY PERSONNEL.

MYCROFT (*setting down his newspaper*). How did he get in here – How did this man get in here?

WATSON. Holmes, what are we doing here!?

SHERLOCK. Delay the sentencing in the Sholto case!

SHERLOCK *has stolen someone's drink.*

MYCROFT. This is a jobless drug-addict trespasser – Get him out!

SHERLOCK *grabs a paper from someone and evades security as he calls over the commotion:*

SHERLOCK. 'Mystery Body Discovered Behind Locked Doors!' 'Strange headline,' I thought, 'with the world as it is.' But then I saw that he was a civil servant and it hit me! 'Mycroft's involved' –

MYCROFT. Raving lunatic – Get him out!

SHERLOCK. Which means it's sensitive!

SECURITY *finally manage to get hold* SHERLOCK *and* WATSON.

MYCROFT. Gentlemen, I can only apologise on behalf of my troubled, little brother.

WATSON. *He's* your brother!?

SHERLOCK. Embarrassing, isn't it – MYCROFT! (*Being dragged away.*) Delay the sentencing in the Sholto case and I'll get your Top Secret Plans back!

Having just taken a sip, MYCROFT *spits out his tea.*

MYCROFT. There are no missing Top Secret Plans!

Everyone is looking at MYCROFT.

Perhaps if we give him some space, he'll recover his senses. Terribly sorry.

As MYCROFT *empties the room and waves off* SECURITY, WATSON *straightens himself out and* SHERLOCK *finishes a half-eaten rice pudding that he has discovered.*

WATSON. But Holmes? This is a whole separate case –

SHERLOCK. We need more time!

MYCROFT (*alone now*). Delaying the case of that Sholto murderess is impossible –

SHERLOCK. This décor is impossible, slowing down court proceedings / on the other hand.

MYCROFT. / She killed a knight of the realm *and* his heir.

SHERLOCK. I thought you were the one who got things done in government.

MYCROFT. Who else do you imagine expedited her case?

WATSON. You ? But Mary's innocent, you're interfering with a tried and tested system –

MYCROFT. This *is* the system – You must be his doctor.

WATSON. Sorry, 'His' doctor?

MYCROFT. This is the largest Empire the world has ever seen. The battlefronts aren't only at the frontiers but everywhere. All the time. And the only thing keeping it all from collapse is this! The Big Show! The performance of total control. British superiority – militarily, organisationally, economically – is the biggest deterrent we have, so the murder of key figures by an immigrant… It shakes the scenery.

WATSON. But Mary didn't do it –

MYCROFT. Irrelevant. People think she did and the show must go on.

SHERLOCK. A little speech and two helpings of rice pudding, you're nervous.

MYCROFT. I like rice pudding.

SHERLOCK. When you're stressed.

MYCROFT. I'm not stressed –

SHERLOCK. If I'd lost some Top Secret Plans, I'd be stressed too –

MYCROFT. That woman is being held with the political prisoners at Wormwood Scrubs – It is out of my hands.

SHERLOCK. Shame. Good luck getting your plans back. / Watson, let's go.

MYCROFT. / The greatest minds in government are working on this, Sherlock, with all the resources we have. I placed that article to panic the culprit into error not invite you out from wherever you've been hiding as if you could ever be the solution to anything!

SHERLOCK. Still stopped me leaving though, didn't you?

MYCROFT. Merely to amuse myself at the very idea of you being able to recover our Top Secret Plans… bugger.

SHERLOCK. Knew it. We only need until the tide changes. Deal?

MYCROFT. Sorry, is he high?

WATSON. Very. Does it matter?

MYCROFT. Deal. I may be able to create a momentary deferment but there's no way you'll get them back –

SHERLOCK. Leave that to me. Oh, and we'll need the fastest boat you can find. What are those plans for again?

MYCROFT. If I told you, Sherlock, not only would we all be killed but this room would be purged with fire and the building turned into a Boots.

SHERLOCK. A weapon, then.

MYCROFT (*scoffing*). What!?

SHERLOCK. Why else would you choose such violent imagery?

MYCROFT. Hardly conclusive –

SHERLOCK. No, but your terrible acting is. So the civil servant stole the plans for some weapon –

MYCROFT. Not just 'some weapon', Sherlock, if that thing were to fall into the… bugger.

SHERLOCK. I was always better at this than you.

MYCROFT. Better at putting things back together than building them.

SHERLOCK. Which is why you're the one with the glittering career and I have a Final Rent warning in my pocket. Why did he take them?

MYCROFT. We believe the civil servant intended to sell them –

WATSON. Arthur Cadogan-West. His name was in the article.

MYCROFT. If those Top Secret Plans were to get to a country that could afford to build that weapon… The world order as we know it will end.

SHERLOCK. Show me where they were stolen from.

MYCROFT *leads as the* STAFF *of The Diogenes Club work around* SHERLOCK *and* WATSON *to create…*

WATSON (*grabbing a moment*). Holmes, if that boat gets away, Sholto's real killers escape –

SHERLOCK. And Mary will be executed.

WATSON. Is that meant to be reassuring cos it really wasn't –

SHERLOCK. Relax. Mycroft will buy us more time to catch them. Try some rice pudding.

…a bustling government building, desks, harried people with papers and too much work.

MYCROFT. Welcome to The Archive. Arthur had worked here for years, never attracted attention or comment. Sat here…

A desk, filing cabinets and a trolley full of files. SHERLOCK *sits in Arthur's chair and searches the drawers as* WATSON *begins flipping through the filing cabinet.*

…all day, every day, checking the fine print and details. Last Monday –

WATSON. Sewers, underground, Wormwood Scrubs – (*Removing a folder.*) Oooo, Tower Bridge!

MYCROFT. Most of London's major building projects will have passed across his desk. Last Monday –

WATSON. But this folder's empty.

MYCROFT. They all are.

WATSON. Arthur took all of the blueprints?

MYCROFT. As well as –

SHERLOCK. The Top Secret Plans –

MYCROFT. Which were –

SHERLOCK. Kept in the poorly concealed safe over there.

WATSON. Over where? I can't…

Whilst inspecting the desk, SHERLOCK *points and the 'concealed' safe appears on our stage.*

Oh. But it's been blown open.

MYCROFT. A small, expertly applied detonation was heard last Monday.

WATSON. Hang on. (*Retrieving his pad and pencil.*) Yep?

MYCROFT. Shortly before midnight, the guards heard a muffled explosion, they arrived seconds later to find the Top Secret Plans missing.

SHERLOCK. So when were all these trip-wires and pressure plates triggered?

MYCROFT. Only *after* the explosion.

WATSON. So the guards got here, the plans were gone and there was no one around?

SHERLOCK. No open windows? Doors?

MYCROFT. Nothing. At night, everything is sealed, locked and alarmed and there are more guards here than at the palace. There is simply no way in or out of The Archive – It's one of the most secure places in the entire kingdom.

SHERLOCK. So the break-in was on Monday evening, correct?

WATSON. But Arthur's body wasn't discovered until the Wednesday morning.

SHERLOCK. Was Arthur here on Tuesday?

MYCROFT. He signed in for work as usual, by all accounts he spent his day working and filing as usual. He signed out at his regular hour only to reappear dead at Aldgate station having apparently been murdered that evening.

SHERLOCK. There's really no way in?

SHERLOCK *begins to examine the trolley.*

MYCROFT. None, it's impossible to access.

SHERLOCK. Impossible?

MYCROFT. A degree of ventilation is necessary to keep the documents from rotting but only someone –

SHERLOCK. – with a comprehensive understanding of this building's structure might know how?

DOMINGO *emerges from among the files on the trolley and climbs on top of it.*

MYCROFT. You're suggesting an accomplice?

WATSON. An accomplice that Arthur helped find a way into the ventilation system.

SHERLOCK *finds scuffs and marks around nearby desks and walls, and traces a line with his hand.*

MYCROFT. Even then, with all the pressure plates and trip-wires, there is no way to cross this space without raising the alarm.

DOMINGO *follows the line – crossing the space without raising the alarm – Parkour? Tightrope? Magic? – until he reaches the safe.*

It's a fine theory, Sherlock. Far-fetched but –

WATSON. Brilliant.

MYCROFT. But how did he disappear? Immediately *after* the alarm was sounded?

SHERLOCK. That's the easy part.

DOMINGO *blows the safe – the alarm sounds – he grabs the Top Secret Plans and heads for the trolley. As he goes, his red jacket catches on an edge of the exploded safe and rips. SHERLOCK picks up the scrap as DOMINGO scrambles over the plates and trip-wires to conceal himself inside the trolley.*

We see the GUARDS *arrive and discover the safe but no trace of* DOMINGO. *They cordon it off.*

WATSON. So the thief didn't leave until –

SHERLOCK. The day *after* the robbery. Arthur signed in and…

ARTHUR *arrives and places his files from his desk – the ones* WATSON *declared were empty – into the trolley and leaves, pushing the* DOMINGO *trolley out.*

…simply trundled him out.

MYCROFT. Then why did the thief bother to kill Arthur?

WATSON. To cover his tracks, obviously.

SHERLOCK. No. If no one had found his body, we'd be chasing *Arthur* / instead of whoever really did all this.

MYCROFT. / Instead of whoever really did all this.

SHERLOCK. We're missing something.

MYCROFT. At least we know the Top Secret Plans haven't left London yet.

WATSON. How?

MYCROFT. Because we're not yet at war.

SHERLOCK. Arthur's body, who found it?

MYCROFT. The first shift, unlocking the station. Hadn't been there before so –

WATSON. What, magically appeared over night?

SHERLOCK. We need to see the body.

The morgue forms around them and ARTHUR*'s body, under a sheet, is rolled in.*

MYCROFT. Okay. But be warned, the heat this summer's made it hard to keep the bodies fresh.

SHERLOCK. Morgue, please!

MYCROFT leaves and SHERLOCK *lifts the sheet revealing* ARTHUR*'s putrescent body – not the face.* WATSON *and* SHERLOCK *can't help but react.*

Watson. This leg break. Before or *after* death?

WATSON. Minimal contusions, likely *after* death.

With a sickening crack, WATSON *adjusts the leg.* WATSON *goes to a box of clothes.*

SHERLOCK. These scratches haven't clotted –

WATSON (*checking a box*). Also *after* death, then. He could have been dragged or thrown *after* being killed… Holmes, there's a wedding ring here.

SHERLOCK. Surely you can afford to buy one.

WATSON. But Arthur had played his part. He'd done what was asked. Why did he have to die?

SHERLOCK. Because morality is a lie, Watson. But why did they let him be found. (*Holding* ARTHUR*'s arm.*) What's this? Ink?

WATSON (*inspecting*). A child's scribble, I'd say.

SHERLOCK. Why hasn't he washed it off?

WATSON. Cos. Holmes, this was a person, a fully aware, loved, person.

SHERLOCK. Anyone *fully aware* wouldn't have inflicted this world on a child. They would have overcome their base animal instincts and refrained from yanking another consciousness out of nonexistence into a universe of suffering – Anything that matches this?

SHERLOCK *passes* WATSON *the red scrap of material he found in the previous scene.*

WATSON. You know, Holmes, there are good people in the world and we are clearly more than animals, we have community, developed nations, love – (*Re. the cloth.*) No match here.

SHERLOCK. A fairytale to excuse ruthless exploitation. Cause of death?

WATSON *hobbles over to investigate the body.*

WATSON. This fairytale lifted me out of the life to which I'd been born. Gave me a schooling, a place in society –

SHERLOCK. And you were so grateful, you took a bullet for it.

WATSON. If you'd *seen* the reality out there – In the darkness, Holmes, that's where the light matters most. There was good – Yes, goodness, even out there so I happen to believe in that fairytale –

SHERLOCK. You also believe you're still injured, doesn't make it true –

WATSON. What do you want from me?

SHERLOCK. Honesty! Choosing the loved one isn't selfless, it's just trying to win something else. This place, that war, it's under your skin, Watson –

WATSON. I injected you with that stuff to help *you* –

SHERLOCK. Cos you needed something – That's the logic of Empire, it's all for your own good –

WATSON. Do you not trust that I'm your friend?

SHERLOCK. No such thing. There's no such thing. Same as 'trust' and 'love', Watson, they're coping mechanisms. You can't let anyone in. Not friends, not Mary, not accomplices – look what happens when you make that mistake.

SHERLOCK *whips off the sheet covering* ARTHUR's *face – it is contorted into a horrific smile.*

WATSON. Found the cause of death.

Using a hankie, WATSON *plucks a thorn from* ARTHUR's *neck.*

SHERLOCK. Is that – ?

WATSON. It's the same poison that killed the Sholtos. Which means / it's the same case.

SHERLOCK. / It's the same case.

WATSON (*passing the hankie-thorn to* SHERLOCK). But, if Arthur was killed by the same people, and they've got both the treasure and the Top Secret Plans –

SHERLOCK. They could build the Weapon.

NANCY appears, out of breath, struggling against POLICE:

NANCY. Mr Holmes! Get off me! / (*Fujianese.*) 大頭呆！[*Tāi-thâu-tai*!] [You massive bell-end!]

SHERLOCK (*sequestering the hankie-thorn*). / She's with us! It's okay – She's one of my irregulars.

NANCY. It's *The Aurora*, it's ready to leave a dock just north of here.

WATSON. Quickly! To the river!

WATSON leads SHERLOCK in a race through London – a blur of coats, mud, smog and umbrellas.

Out of the way! Coming through!

Dockworkers, boxes, a glimpse of a brightly coloured snake and a whirl of a tarpaulin before they jump aboard a boat! A POLICE BOATMAN had been snoozing when they arrive:

We're with Mycroft Holmes – Start those bloody engines!

SHERLOCK. There she is! Already ahead of us!

Water, steam, heat and the `effort of shovelling coal.*

WATSON. Pile it on, man! *After* that boat! They're pulling away – Here!

WATSON grabs a shovel and starts to throw coals on the fire.

SHERLOCK. That's it! We're gaining on them!

Spotting something, WATSON pulls SHERLOCK down. Gunshots and bullets whizz by.

WATSON. You're the only one capable of arguing Mary's case – You stay down!

SHERLOCK helps WATSON up and pick-pockets his revolver – WATSON resumes shovelling!

POLICE. They're headed for Tower Bridge, sir. It's not safe –

WATSON. To hell with it, *after* them!

The boat lurches, girders pass perilously close, metal screams against metal.

POLICE. But the scaffolding, sir –

SHERLOCK (*wielding the gun like a lunatic*). Just do as he says!

It's all sweat, heat and cold Thames water at Regent's Park as SHERLOCK takes aim.

WATSON. Holmes, no, we need them alive – NO!

BANG! Things suddenly calm down. WATSON snatches his revolver from SHERLOCK.

SHERLOCK. Should still be alive.

WATSON. Bring us alongside, be prepared for savagery.

When the police boat bumps against The Aurora, WATSON goes full soldier as he jumps aboard. SMALL, grinning and bleeding over the familiar treasure chest in his lap, his shoulder injury making it impossible for him to lift his Cigarettes Laurens.

SMALL. Got a light, mate?

SHERLOCK and POLICE follow WATSON aboard. WATSON hands SHERLOCK his matches from earlier.

WATSON (*to POLICE*). Search the boat, the accomplice should be here somewhere.

Over the following, POLICE search The Aurora as SHERLOCK sets SMALL up with a fag and lights it.

SMALL. May as well be searching for smoke in the fog.

SHERLOCK. He's gone?

SMALL. You're chasing a shadow, mate. A feeling, something out in the long grass you've always known would come for you.

WATSON. What's your name?

SMALL. On these shores, Private Small of the Third Buffs.

WATSON (*taking back his matches*). Right, Small, an innocent woman's fate is in your hands. So these men are gonna arrest you and then you're gonna confess to Sholto's murder.

SMALL. Wasn't me what done for him.

WATSON. Then you're gonna state exactly what happened under oath.

SMALL. Can't. Got a pact.

SMALL *shows his hand and the memory of* MORSTAN, SHOLTO *and* TONGA *making their blood oaths appear around him.*

SHERLOCK. The pact that Morstan and Sholto broke.

SMALL. Weren't no better than a child's promise to them. But then, what's in here, it's dark magic. Shows you a future, summons something up from inside you what you didn't know was there – Moment we opened it I knew rules, codes, honour, all just words, just air.

MORSTAN *shoots* SMALL, *then strikes* TONGA *with the butt.* SHOLTO *grabs the chest and they leave.*

SHERLOCK. Your accomplice, what's his name?

SMALL. Dunno, well, not his real name. There were these carts, they called 'em 'Tangar' or 'Tonga', the lads used to make him pull 'em to save their horses. The name stuck.

Recovered from his injury, TONGA *stands.*

SHERLOCK. Tonga.

SMALL. He'd been servant to the Empress. They were shipping her off in secret, we were making a deal so's we could sail with her but –

SHERLOCK. Morstan and Sholto left you both to the mutineers. But Tonga saved you. Why?

TONGA *lifts* SMALL *and, as* SMALL *speaks, his story is recreated through the power of movement!*

SMALL. Dunno. Come 'round at sea, on a little merchant ship. We helped where we could and they took us around the colonies until –

SHERLOCK. You could follow the treasure.

SMALL. Got by with a few shows, bit of busking, me and the 'curiosity' that he was, a few rupees here, dinar there, lira, pesos, francs – But each step closer to this treasure, he's changing. Catch him listening to things he shouldn't understand. Whispering to himself when he thinks I'm drunk or sleeping. He's making sounds like counting in his sleep, like counting coins, making plans, I start having to beat him, it's like his face, the bones in it have moved, he's taller –

SHERLOCK. Until you arrived here –

SMALL. And took back what was ours. (*The treasure is back with* SMALL.) But by then what I knew of Tonga was smoke.

TONGA *has disappeared and* SMALL *is back in the boat, finishing his smoke and bleeding.*

SHERLOCK. He killed Sholto.

SMALL. What killed Sholto was his own greed.

SHERLOCK. And Thaddeus?

SMALL (*chuckling*). Not wrong to profit from wrongdoing, then? Convenient.

WATSON (*reaching for the chest*). No time for this, let's get it in front of a judge –

SMALL *'s laughter suddenly changes to growling and barking like a dog.*

There's no way out, Small. Do some good!

SMALL. Good?! I was a soldier. I've more than earned this – Least let me take a last look at it.

SHERLOCK. So Tonga did all this only to leave it with you?

SMALL *opens the box, a click and something hits his wrist.*

SMALL. Empty!?

Confused, SMALL lets the chest tumble and plucks the thorn from his skin. He starts to chuckle, but as WATSON speaks, his laughter turns to screaming pain.

WATSON. No! A knife! We have to bleed the poison – Knife! Mary needs his testimony!

SMALL *'s face gradually contorts into a horrible smile as he spasms and dies.*

SHERLOCK. It's too late, Watson. We have to get *after* Tonga, he can't have gone far – find the slave that belonged to this man!

WATSON. Sherlock… Small was the slave.

SHERLOCK. What?

WATSON. He did everything Tonga wanted, broke him out of his cell, got him off the colonies to Pondicherry Lodge and as soon as he could –

SHERLOCK. – took the treasure. This is all Tonga's plan – Why didn't I see it?

WATSON. Wherever he is, he'll be weighed down. He could have jumped off at the bridge back there – Full-steam ahead, lads!

SHERLOCK. No. Tonga was never on this boat. He used Small as a distraction.

WATSON. From what?

A flare explodes in the sky over London.

POLICE. That's an emergency signal, we're needed on shore.

SHERLOCK. Watson, Arthur's desk, the blueprints that were missing.

WATSON. Yeah, building projects, the underground, Tower Bridge – Why?

SHERLOCK. What if the Secret Plans were also a distraction. That signal, what does it mean?

POLICE. Prison break, sir.

WATSON. Wormwood Scrubs. Political prisoners.

Distant police whistles and sirens, monkey or hyenas or people screaming everything builds…

SHERLOCK. This is bigger than we thought.

End of Act One.

ACT TWO

A roar, human or animal we can't tell, brings us into a sweaty, humid, London-fever dream. Voices among a range of animal calls…

SHERLOCK. This is bigger than we thought.

> SHERLOCK *stands among creatures in the haze – loping, prowling, dancing – part hallucination, part the nightmare of every privileged Englishman living in the age of colonial control!*

TONGA (*Hindustani*). *Kasam. Jaan ki kasam. Yeh vada kabhi nahi tootega* [Swear first. A blood oath. An unbreakable oath.]

SMALL. You shall be hunted and dogged 'til your last breath. All the devils and demons and creatures of the earth at your heels chasing you down to hell.

TOMMO. A creature they say sings instead of speaks.

BILL. Market's flooded with cheap opium…

MARY. The great work of the Empire and men like Dr Watson has improved their countries tenfold. London is full.

THADDEUS. Help me liberate that treasure once more!

SMALL. The thing out in the long grass you've always known is coming just never known when.

WATSON. We thought we were hunting them, they were hunting us all along.

MYCROFT. This is the largest Empire the world has ever seen. The battlefronts aren't only at the frontiers but / everywhere all the time.

SMALL *is growling, barking.*

Somewhere, among the cacophony of animal and human voices, a JUDGE *speaks from the bench:*

JUDGE. Madam, you are here to be sentenced! The only term for you was coined for those who led 'The Reign of Terror'. You are this great nation's first and, God willing, last *terrorist.*

MYCROFT (*voiceover*). And the only thing keeping it all from all from / collapse is…

JUDGE. / The embodiment of the real threat to / this Empire –

MYCROFT (*voiceover*). / The Big Show!

JUDGE. The threat from within.

TONGA (*voiceover, Hindustani*). *Bharosa.* [Trust.]

Around SHERLOCK *a courthouse forms,* WATSON *rushing to intercept* MARY *on her way to the dock:*

WATSON. Mary! It's a show, this system just needs to tell your story –

The JUDGE *competing with a raucous crowd of animal-like cries as he places a black cap on his head:*

JUDGE. Order! Madam! I hereby sentence you –

WATSON. Your honour, allow me to speak on her behalf! This lady's story begins on the dark edges of this Empire, a place of unimaginable –

ALL. ORDER!!

MARY *stands in the dock, handcuffed, between two* POLICE *with animal heads.*

JUDGE. At dawn, Madam, you shall be hanged by the neck until you are dead!

Outcry and uproar. MARY *faints. The animal heads are gone. We have landed firmly in a London courthouse full of* POLICE, *fevered* PRESS *and grieving* ALLIES *of the Sholtos. Amid the chaos,* WATSON *throws himself at* MYCROFT.

WATSON. Mycroft! We had a deal! An innocent woman's life is at stake!!

SHERLOCK. Mycroft, listen to us.

POLICE, MYCROFT, WATSON *and* SHERLOCK – *in a daze – are suddenly in a quieter side room.*

WATSON. You said you'd slow it down – Now, they're about to hang her!?

MYCROFT. Well, dawn's still a few hours / away –

WATSON (*launching for* MYCROFT). RAGH!

POLICE (*wielding a club*). Get back!

The POLICE *hold* WATSON *back.*

WATSON. Is this what I fought for!? This system of – ?!

MYCROFT. That war isn't over! Stolen Top Secret Plans, a mass prison break – It's an open invitation to our enemies to attack and you're worried about your lady friend – !?

WATSON. About the truth, you / posh bastard!

POLICE. / Control yourself, sir!

SHERLOCK. Mycroft, it's all connected, I just –

MYCROFT. This Tonga thing – Sherlock, you've got no proof! This is far bigger than you and your theories, you are a pistol in an artillery war – Sixty-one of our most classified political prisoners – Socialists, Anarchists, Ex-Heads of State – All escape from our most secure facility days *after* the Secret Plans are stolen and you tell me it's all the work of one escaped slave!?

WATSON. But it is! The poison was the same – Holmes, tell him! Make the case!

SHERLOCK.…

MYCROFT. My sympathies, Doctor, you put your faith in a suicidal lunatic.

WATSON. Mycroft, what do we have to do to save Mary?

MYCROFT. Prove his Tonga theory. Get the Secret Plans back. And find that stolen treasure. Quickly.

The POLICE *and* MYCROFT *re-enter the fray.*

WATSON. For God's sake – You've put Mary on a one-track journey to the scaffold, Mycroft! One track and no hope of hitting those – the levers that change the train's direction –

SHERLOCK. Points.

WATSON. No hope of hitting the / points, Mycroft you did that!

SHERLOCK. / Poooooiiints.

WATSON. Holmes, why are you just saying 'points'!?

The POLICE *and* MYCROFT *are being subsumed by chaos as the courthouse is fast becoming a riot:*

SHERLOCK (*suddenly alert*). Mycroft! Arthur's body! Was it on the platform or the tracks?

MYCROFT. Tracks. (*Leaving.*) Eastbound!

WATSON. Holmes, what do we – ?

SHERLOCK *is gone.*

CONDUCTOR. Westbound Metropolitan line. All aboard! (*Blows whistle.*)

The chaos snaps into a crowded train carriage – SHERLOCK *in the midst of the* COMMUTERS *–* WATSON *only just jumps aboard before departure.*

WATSON. He said East – Why are we – Where are we even going?

Beside SHERLOCK, *a* COMMUTER*'s paper bears the headline: 'Sholto Murderess Set to Hang!'*

SHERLOCK. Arthur's leg-break and contusions, are they consistent with a fall?

WATSON. Arthur the – ?

SHERLOCK. Dead man who helped steal the Secret Plans, yes, one break and a few contusions –

WATSON. A short fall, yes, but *after* he'd been killed – How is this meant to save Mary?

SHERLOCK. Our best bet for finding Tonga is finding where he murdered Arthur. Is it me or is there a bit of an atmosphere?

The COMMUTERS *are worrying about this pair of lunatics.*

WATSON. But Arthur's body was found back at Aldgate, we're heading West.

SHERLOCK. We're going from where his body was dumped to where he was killed.

WATSON. So, he wasn't killed at Aldgate station? But (*Indicating someone's paper.*) 'Mystery Body Discovered Behind Locked Doors.' How did it get there, then?

SHERLOCK. It was found by the first shift of the day which means there was only one way in.

WATSON. On a train? I'd like to think a bloodied corpse might have attracted *some* attention…

SHERLOCK *is pointing up –* ARTHUR*'s body appears above them, held up by* COMMUTERS.

Ooooon the roof!

SHERLOCK. Of the last Westbound train of the evening before. Which took it far away from the murder scene before –

The train lurches and ARTHUR *is thrown off the roof and out of sight.* WATSON *retrieves his pad.*

WATSON. – it bumped over the points at Aldgate and fell.

SHERLOCK. Hence the leg-break, scratches and being found behind locked doors.

WATSON (*pausing*). But doesn't that mean it could only have been placed somewhere, where it couldn't have gone over any of the other points on the line?

SHERLOCK. Exactly, the body had to be placed on the roof of that train somewhere before Aldgate points but *after* the previous set of points. Which is why we're on our way back along the journey the body made until we go over –

WATSON. Another set of –

The train lurches again.

– points. Amazing. (*Writing.*) Just...

SHERLOCK. Not now, Watson. Come on.

SHERLOCK *forces a door open whilst the train is still moving.*

CONDUCTOR. Oi! What you doing? You can't get off here! Train's still moving –

SHERLOCK *jumps off the train and rolls over the gravel.* WATSON *follows and the train rumbles away as* WATSON *crawls to find his pad and pen.*

SHERLOCK. For the body to have travelled as far as it did, it would have to have been carefully placed... Watson?

WATSON. Yuuurp... Revolver... dug into my guts.

SHERLOCK. Do you see anywhere high enough?

WATSON. Holmes. What makes you think Tonga will still be there?

SHERLOCK. What other lead do we have?

WATSON. Mary's only got until dawn... we haven't got time to get this wrong.

SHERLOCK. I know that.

WATSON. What about Wormwood Scrubs? Maybe there's something there? Some clue or –

SHERLOCK. No, we have to get ahead. Here, this place backs straight onto the –

WATSON. Train.

SHERLOCK. Exactly, we just need to –

WATSON. Holmes!

WATSON *grabs* SHERLOCK *just as a train whooshes by dangerously close leaving them…*

Jesus Christ! Look… I need to know you're not… that you're okay. Of sound mind.

Beat.

SHERLOCK. That show. It was in the paper, the woman who'd lost her ticket.

…a huge sign reading 'The Wonders of the Empire' and a DOOR LADY *sitting in a ticket booth.*

DOOR LADY. Shilling each for the late show, gents.

SHERLOCK. How much would it cost to place an advert for a lost ticket?

WATSON. More than a shilling.

SHERLOCK. Right, so why shell out for an advert instead of just buying another ticket? Two, please.

WATSON *pays.*

DOOR LADY. Enjoy the show!

FIREBREATHERS *scorch the air! The circus surrounds* SHERLOCK *and* WATSON. *Music, sword swallowing,* JUGGLERS, CONTORTIONISTS. WATSON *and* SHERLOCK *push through the* CROWD.

RINGMASTER. The Great British Empire has spread across the world like arms embracing the planet, drawing into Britannia's bosom the weirdest, wildest and strangest folk. (*During the* TUMBLERS.) From the farthest reaches of the Empire, tamed, trained and tempted by our pie n' mash, the dangerous Savages of Siam!

TUMBLERS *cross the space but then the* SWORD-SWALLOWER *grabs one of them.*

Careful, now! The Sultan of the Sword is a hot-blooded heathen! But… since Britannia took him in, he's become one of us! See, he's alright really.

The SWORD-SWALLOWER *releases the* TUMBLER – *Waheey! – and now his act begins:*

Witness, the Brother of the Blade himself, make a supper of his sabre!

The SWORD-SWALLOWER *makes way for the* STRONG MAN.

And now, dragged – willingly – from the quarries of Queensland, fed on British beef and bold endeavour, Atlas of the Antipodes!

The STRONG MAN *does his thing but leaves his 'incredibly heavy' weight on the stage.*

POGO, *a clown, cycles on to retrieve the 'weight' – revealing that it's fake! – what a dork!*

Ah, come on! He's a continental catastrophe, ladies and gents, as bothersome as the Balkans from whence he hails, the master of muddles, the foreign fuss himself – Oh, good, he's gone.

The FIRE-BREATHER *starts his act.*

Hark! For from the smoke-wreathed alleys of the murky medina, we welcome the ember-eyed enigma himself, Professor Vulcanus! Watch as he makes bold with the blaze! Deals with destruction! Enjoys the inferno!

SHERLOCK *and* WATSON *have made it to the wings of the stage where* AUDREY *stands with a snake. A singer continuing the show as they have this scene:*

SINGER (*singing*).
We're a prison break
You're forgotten mistake

The cages are empty
The creatures are here
Dancing among you
My tongue smells the fear
The animals escaped the zoo
Now the one who's caged is you.

AUDREY. You meant to be back 'ere?

WATSON. / No, we were actually just –

SHERLOCK (*doing a voice*). / Yes, RSPCA, concerned about your animals.

AUDREY. What animals? We've only got Cleopatra, here.

SHERLOCK. Right, where'd you get her from?

AUDREY. *He* was born with us. Always stay near the nest, snakes do.

SHERLOCK. What's the furthest they'll travel in their lifetime?

AUDREY. Not further'n a mile – 'Ere, is this a test?

SHERLOCK. Yes, and I'll need some paperwork, now if you could just let / us do our work –

RINGMASTER. / And now for our long-awaited finale!

A group of TUMBLERS *push by as they prepare for their entrance.* WATSON *notices that one of them has a ragged tail to his red jacket.*

SHERLOCK *looks just in time to see that the scrap matches the damaged costume as the* TUMBLERS *run, flip and dance out onto the stage – clearly the kind of moves that would have helped someone avoid alarms and pressure plates in a secure facility.*

Steel your nerves for supple as panthers, swift as musket-fire, the savages are returned! Watch as they fly through the London air as they would their native jungles. Where they eat what they catch and one man is their chief.

The show dips to a drum-roll as DOMINGO *performs the same extraordinary feats he did in The Archive earlier and prepares to take his bow.*

Ladies and gentlemen, the great Domingo! Though he speaks no English, Domingo wishes to share his gratitude to our great nation in his mother tongue –

DOMINGO *spots* SHERLOCK.

DOMINGO (*broad London accent*). Fuckin' 'ell! Sorry, mate, gotta go.

DOMINGO *makes a run for it –* SHERLOCK *and* WATSON *spring into action.*

RINGMASTER (*hushed*). / I'll knock your bloody –

SHERLOCK (*directing him to cut* DOMINGO *off*). Watson!

RINGMASTER (*louder*). Music! Ladies and gentlemen, it's all part of the show!

SHERLOCK (*directing him to cut* DOMINGO *off*). Watson!

The show resumes under the force of will of the RINGMASTER. *But as he speaks,* DOMINGO *cuts one way and then another, trapped between* SHERLOCK *and* WATSON, *and things start to go wrong.* TUMBLERS *fall,* FIRE-BREATHERS *burn,* SWORD-SWALLOWERS *choke.*

RINGMASTER. Do not be afraid, everyone! Everything is under contro–

WATSON (*firing his revolver into the air*). STOP THAT MAN!

Screams and pandemonium. DOMINGO *evades* SHERLOCK *with his athleticism.* WATSON *is trying to get ahead but the* CROWD *prevents him.* DOMINGO *gets to the top first and dives out of the window.*

SHERLOCK *bolts back through the theatre in the opposite direction.*

JUGGLER (*Italian*). *Che diavolo stai facendo*?! [What the hell are you doing?!]

RINGMASTER. 'Ere, what's your game, / scaring everyone off?

CLOWN. / Yeah, not funny, mate!

DOOR-LADY (*Punjabi*). *Iha tū kī kara rihā haiṁ*?! *Ithē baaūka calā rihā haiṁ*! [What the hell are you doing?! Firing a gun in here!]

RINGMASTER. Are you police? There's a riot brewing out there, why you in here for?!

WATSON (*trying to get away*). That man's a dangerous criminal.

AUDREY. Domingo? He's a tumbler!

WATSON. Domingo is not his real name!

CLOWN. You think I'm really called Pogo?

RINGMASTER (*to the* FIRE-BREATHER). No, no, no – Save it!

A blast of flame and DOMINGO *flies through the space, leaping and tumbling until his path blocked.*

SHERLOCK (*breathless*). You tried – Led me – Wrong way –

DOMINGO. Let me get by.

SHERLOCK. Down – Regent's Canal? Can't.

DOMINGO. You said about that treasure being worth more than money to the people it was stolen from. Not being free wealth but stolen history –

SHERLOCK. Brixton. You pointed the way to the dock, set us on Small's trail.

DOMINGO. You know all of this is built on blood. 'All unethical.'

SHERLOCK *blocks* DOMINGO's *path.*

SHERLOCK. That was – The pub – With the Irregulars –

DOMINGO (*drawing a knife*). I don't want to hurt you.

SHERLOCK. Like you hurt that civil servant *after* he helped you steal those Top Secret Plans?

DOMINGO. It's war here. Same as in Sudan or anywhere. Now, move or be moved.

SHERLOCK. You're trapped, I need you to hand over –

SHERLOCK *tries to block* DOMINGO*'s path but* DOMINGO *swiftly and expertly has him beaten.*

DOMINGO. Why are you trying to stop us?

SHERLOCK. 'Us'?

BANG! DOMINGO *collapses onto* SHERLOCK.

WATSON. Holmes!? Are you okay?

WATSON, *having struggled after* DOMINGO, *pockets his revolver and starts to clamber down.*

SHERLOCK. How many of you are there?

DOMINGO (*dying*). This rebellion's everywhere. In everyone. Even you.

SHERLOCK....me?

With his last efforts, DOMINGO *gives* SHERLOCK *a bright red envelope: The Top Secret Plans.*

DOMINGO. Do the right thing.

Some shouting from off and a police whistle. A CROWD *beginning to gather around the body.*

WATSON (*to* CROWD). Don't worry, I'm working on behalf of the Crown. Holmes, what did he say? Did he tell you about the treasure?

SHERLOCK. He might have done if you hadn't shot him.

WATSON. He was about to kill you! A 'thank you' wouldn't go amiss. (*To* CROWD.) This man was a known thief and murderer named Tonga.

SHERLOCK. No, he wasn't.

WATSON. Please alert any police in the – Sorry, *not* Tonga?

SHERLOCK. Sorry, old bean.

WATSON. Oh, God… I just killed a gymnast.

SHERLOCK *starts roughly removing* DOMINGO*'s red jacket.*

SHERLOCK. He was part of it.

WATSON. What are you doing?

SHERLOCK. Royal Engineers' tattoo. Explains how he blew open the safe.

WATSON. No, leave him – Wait, 'part of it'? Part of what?

SHERLOCK. The Conspiracy, Watson. This was a foot soldier, we need the mastermind. (*Helping* WATSON *into* DOMINGO*'s red coat.*) Now, put this on and let's not hang around, eh?

WATSON. Why? I just killed a British soldier, Sherlock. On our own streets. Oh, God. I should turn myself in.

SHERLOCK. And give up on Mary? You can make amends later, right now we need to get to wherever he was headed.

SHERLOCK *sets off, away from the body and along Regent's Canal.* WATSON *follows.*

Unrest in London is growing, so the London that passes by now is angry and hot-tempered.

WATSON. So, you're saying that – That Domingo was –

SHERLOCK. Part of something bigger. He served in Sudan, likely the Balloon Section and he's been trailing us since the beginning – They're organised and they're winning, Watson.

WATSON. Woah, Holmes, slow down – A conspiracy? A mastermind? Isn't this all a bit – ?

SHERLOCK. Isn't it, just?

They pass a VENDOR *selling newspapers:*

VENDOR. Sholto killer set to hang for double-murder!

SHERLOCK *gives* WATSON *the Top Secret Plans and takes a paper.*

WATSON. But Holmes… these are the Secret Plans! We have to get these to Mycroft!

SHERLOCK. Domingo was on his way somewhere to meet someone and we need to find out who.

WATSON. What? No, Holmes, Mary's only got until sunrise –

SHERLOCK. The only way to save her now is to prove I'm right about all of it!

VENDOR. It's not free, mate.

WATSON *pays for the paper that* SHERLOCK *is reading as he walks.*

WATSON. Let's just use the leverage we have! For all we know Tonga could be –

SHERLOCK. Shhh – I'm working out where they were going to meet.

WATSON. From the newspaper?

SHERLOCK. This bit, read it out.

SHERLOCK *gives* WATSON *the paper and takes back the Top Secret Plans.*

WATSON (*reading*). 'To the gentleman who found my lost ticket. Meet *after* the show at peace with formalities. Yours, Crusoe.'

SHERLOCK. *After* the show, I assume that's now, given Domingo was in such a rush, but 'At peace with formalities'? Could be payment? The deal? A keyword!

WATSON. Holmes, listen to me –

They are on the move, London streaming by. SHERLOCK *pickpockets and lifts various things from the people and places he passes; a red jacket, make-up, a wig from a bald man…*

SHERLOCK. 'Crusoe' seems more out of place. Six letters, columnar transposition with 'Crusoe' would require four 'X's to make the grid. 'Ticket' might be appropriate given –

WATSON. / Holmes – What are you doing? –

SHERLOCK. It appeared in both messages, but it would need the same thing. Guessing at keywords, Watson, hardly ideal.

WATSON. You're pick-pocketing, stealing – and weirdly good at it.

SHERLOCK. You just summarily executed a man, aren't we in the world of 'the greater good'?

WATSON. He would have killed you –

SHERLOCK. 'To the gentleman who found my lost ticket. Meet *after* the show at peace with formalities. Yours, Crusoe.' The first letter of each word, excluding the keyword and sign-off makes T, T, G, W, F, M, L, T, M, A, T, S, A, P, W, F. Write it down in your little book. Crusoe, the keyword, gives each letter their value. C being third in the alphabet, R being eighteenth, each of those letters indicate a column. So C would amount to – Sit down here.

SHERLOCK *has collected all the bits and pieces he needs. He directs* WATSON *to sit on a bench. Not so far away, a giraffe nibbles at the trees.*

WATSON. Holmes, I don't think you're –

SHERLOCK. Stay still. T, T, G, W doesn't work with Crusoe. Try 'ticket' as the keyword you get –

SHERLOCK *has begun to use everything that he has found and stolen to alter* WATSON*'s appearance.*

T, T, G, W – Nonsense – Still! You have to look like him – Now, quiet! Last letters of each word would make the sequence O, E, N, O, D, Y, T, R, E, S, T, E, H, S /

WATSON. / Holmes, listen to yourself. /

SHERLOCK. / Excluding sign-off gives us values of – of – of –

WATSON. Sherlock Holmes! Don't you think it's possible that you're in the midst of a – a breakdown?

SHERLOCK. Does it matter? We're trying to save the loved one, aren't we? Vowel positions! With 'Crusoe' as the keyword –

WATSON. Wait! Wait, so… this is a coded message meant for Domingo to tell him where to meet, who? Tonga?

SHERLOCK. I didn't say that –

WATSON. So Tonga's signed off 'Crusoe' as per Robinson Crusoe.

SHERLOCK. Who?

WATSON. Robinson Crusoe? Daniel Defoe? A castaway befriends a native – !? This is actually making me feel better about you not reading my book –

SHERLOCK. I don't go in for fashion –

WATSON. No, it's not new. Defoe died over a hundred and fifty years ago.

SHERLOCK. 'At peace'… Where's he buried?

WATSON. Bunhill Fields. It's just along here, it's where Blake and Bunyan and all the non-conformists are buried.

A WORKMAN *carrying a 'Bunhill Fields Burial Ground' sign passes by.*

SHERLOCK. Great! Yes! This is where we'll find our proof. Now, get out there.

WATSON. Looking like I've just stepped out of a Lewis Carroll?

SHERLOCK. Who? Look, take this, the newspaper will sell it. Now, go.

Our CHORUS *have recreated Bunhill Fields.* SHERLOCK *hands* WATSON *a walking stick that he has stolen along the way.*

WATSON. Holmes… Are you sure you're not losing your mind?

SHERLOCK. Can anyone ever be sure of that?

Leaning on his stick, WATSON *hobbles, awkwardly self-aware.*

A few PEOPLE *in the midst of a bickering argument stream by. Someone in grief. Someone running past, holding something that they have clearly looted. And then finally,* LESTRADE *in disguise:*

LESTRADE. Excuse me, I left the house in a rush and don't have my, um –

WATSON (*lighting one of his matches*). Of course.

LESTRADE. Thank you, you see… I'm late for the late show.

WATSON.…the circus? Crusoe. Yes?

LESTRADE…

WATSON (*grabbing him*). C'mere!

POLICE *erupt from the surroundings –* LESTRADE *cuffs* WATSON.

LESTRADE. You're nicked, mate!

WATSON. Lestrade?! No, it's me – / Look, it's me.

LESTRADE. / Oooh, bloody hell. Didn't I tell you to go home?

SHERLOCK (*emerging*). We intercepted the man you're after!

LESTRADE. You en'all!? It's too hot for this nonsense –

SHERLOCK. You'll find him dead, back along Regent's Canal. He attacked and Watson shot him.

LESTRADE. Dead? What is it with you two!? Even his girlfriend's caused a riot. Take 'em both in.

WATSON. No! No, not Holmes! Lestrade, he's working a case –

LESTRADE. That's why we're taking him in. These the Secret Plans, are they?

The POLICE *cuff* SHERLOCK *too.*

SHERLOCK. The person they were meant for should be nearby –

LESTRADE. Get that from the coded message, did you? Well done, mate.

SHERLOCK. That was you?

LESTRADE. We was tipped off. Now, let's get a look at these.

LESTRADE *confidently opens the plan like a paper eagle spreading its wings – but instead of detailed drawings, he finds himself holding a bloodied Union Jack.*

Gor-blimey.

Not far away, a PHOTOGRAPHER *takes a flash-photo.*

Get hands on that flashy git! How'd he know we'd be here? That you two, pricks? Tipping off journalists?

WATSON. Lestrade – listen to me! Holmes is trying to stop something much bigger than your tiny brain could understand and to save the woman you stupidly arrested while you were at it, you absolute –

LESTRADE *slaps* WATSON. *Over the following,* LESTRADE *removes* SHERLOCK *and* WATSON*'s personal effects (revolver, drug paraphernalia and wallet included) as a cell forms around them.*

LESTRADE. Stay here. Spend a bit of time on that book of yours. Maybe it'll be a bit less crap than the first one.

LESTRADE *slaps* WATSON*'s notepad into his chest just before closing the cell doors. He and* SHERLOCK *are locked in with an odd crowd. One of whom is peppered with porcupine spines.*

WATSON. Lestrade! There isn't time for this – LESTRADE!

CELLMATE (*plucking out a spine*). Look, I've actually had quite a tough day. Dunno if you've met a porcupine before, turns out they like their personal space.

WATSON. LESTRADE! An innocent woman is going to hang because of you!

CELLMATE. Could you just keep it down a bit?

WATSON (*back to* SHERLOCK). Holmes, this is a chance to – to just take a breath and – and think. If you work out where Tonga is we can probably convince them to send someone – Domingo must have given you some kind of clue, right? Holmes?

SHERLOCK. …

WATSON (*consulting his pad*). We must be missing something… Indian mutiny, Sholto and Morstan betray Small and Tonga for the treasure that belonged to the last living Mughal heir. Years later, Sholto kills Morstan. Later still, Tonga and Small kill the Sholtos, steal the treasure and Tonga uses Small as a decoy whilst he takes the treasure for himself and breaks sixty-one political prisoners out of Wormwood Scrubs… Right? But then it turns out Tonga's got allies, he and Domingo blackmail Arthur, steal the Top Secret Plans – No, this had to be before. (WATSON *edits his notes.*) They stole the Top Secret Plans before and then Domingo… sets up the sale of the Fake Plans… And tips off Lestrade and the press? But why? Holmes!?

SHERLOCK. Dunno.

WATSON. No, that's not – What's the thing you say? 'Once you've eliminated the impossible, / whatever remains – '

SHERLOCK. / Whatever remains, however improbable, must be the truth.

WATSON. Right. So given Domingo was willing to kill for them, it's safe to say that he didn't know The Plans he had were fake. And he was the only person who could have tipped off the police. Except maybe Tonga? Holmes, why aren't you saying anything? Now's when you tell me I'm wrong and say the thing! Come on, we know who we're *after*, we just don't know where he is or where the Top Secret Plans are or where the treasure is – Christ, we've got –

SHERLOCK. Nothing.

WATSON (*rattling the bars*). HELLO! HELLLOOO!

CELLMATE. Will you give it a rest!?

WATSON. Holmes, you're not trying! You're taking the easy way out and disappearing – I won't let you lose sight of the – the bigger picture – Christ. (*Through the bars.*) HELLO! SOMEONE!

CELLMATE. SHUT UP!

SHERLOCK. Bigger picture – ?

WATSON (*shaking him*). Holmes, do not give up! This is us being – Being more than animal, being better – THINK!

CELLMATE. Mate, I am this close to – !

WATSON. I'M CLOSER! (*Raging, smashing his walking stick to bits.*) I AM THIS BLOODY CLOSE!

POLICE (*returning*). What's all the noise about?

WATSON. YES! You! I need you to do something for me.

As WATSON *seizes this chance to speak,* SHERLOCK *retrieves the poisoned thorn he took earlier on.*

POLICE. I haven't got any fags –

WATSON. I need you to get a message to a man in government called Mycroft.

POLICE. Mycroft Holmes?

WATSON. Yes! Yes, he's probably in crisis talks at Number Ten now or the War Office –

POLICE. So you'll want the nice headed paper then –

WATSON. Yeah, great – Oh, sarcasm, ideal.

POLICE. What's your mate doing?

...just as WATSON *turns around,* SHERLOCK *pushes the thorn into a vein in his arm and collapses.*

WATSON. Moping. Officer, this is a matter of – Holmes?

SHERLOCK *begins to spasm. Somewhere in the distance we can hear music...*

SHERLOCK!

POLICE. I'll get the doctor –

WATSON (*beginning chest compressions*). I am a doctor! If you don't want Mycroft Holmes' brother to die in your custody, get us a taxi to The Jade Dragon, Upper Swandam…

...the music has built by now to drown out WATSON*'s voice and* SHERLOCK *has stood up, leaving* WATSON *trying to revive thin air and walking to...*

...where the fog, dancing and strangeness of an intoxicated dream begins to resolve itself into an exaggerated and strange version of 221B Baker Street. The music resolves into a solitary violin as SHERLOCK *sinks into an armchair and a violin meets his hand.*

MRS HUDSON (*off*). Just up here, love. Few more stairs. Is your leg alright?

Hearing MRS HUDSON *approaching,* SHERLOCK *stops playing.*

WATSON (*off*). Getting there.

MRS HUDSON (*off*). One day we'll learn how to take better care of our veterans, mark my words. Just in here then, love.

MRS HUDSON *enters, clearly surprised not to find* SHERLOCK *here.*

Oh… coulda sworn I heard him.

She is followed by WATSON, *fresh-faced and sprightly compared to the precious scene.*

WATSON. Well… I don't want to do myself out of a cushy deal, Ma'am, this is way more space than I thought.

MRS HUDSON. That's cos I didn't mention you'd be sharing.

WATSON. Okay, well, that makes sense. Hang about, what have you got here? Toxins and – and antidotes – Amazing set-up. Can I ask who you're testing them on?

MRS HUDSON. You can. But I'd have to make up the answer and it wouldn't be convincing.

WATSON. Oh. Not yours, then?

MRS HUDSON. No, love. But I'm starting to think you'll get on. Couple of outsiders.

WATSON. Ah, the accent. I was born in a bit of a rough area, got a scholarship, bit of a mish-mash – Almost all of Britain in one body!

SHERLOCK *gets up from the chair, surprising* MRS HUDSON *and* WATSON *with his presence.*

SHERLOCK. All of Britain, Doctor, and a little lead from a bullet. Afghanistan, I assume.

MRS HUDSON. Say 'hello' to your new roomie.

SHERLOCK. He's not staying.

WATSON. How did you – ?

SHERLOCK. The damage to your shirt collar suggests a stethoscope. The boots, shave, use of the term 'cushy' and concealed revolver suggested the military. Your age suggests Afghanistan and the cost of rent suggests the pension of an invalided officer.

WATSON. All that from looking at me?

SHERLOCK. Observation and deduction – Given the medics weren't involved in much combat, that injury was most likely sustained during the retreat from Kandahar but I didn't want to pry, so –

WATSON. And how did you conclude that I won't be staying?

SHERLOCK. Simple incompatibility.

WATSON. And can you deduce from observation what it was like out there?

SHERLOCK. Afghanistan? Given it was a complete failure, any idiot could tell it wasn't a laugh –

WATSON. Cos you might be very clever but you miss things Things that are obvious to those of us who've lived with more than our heads. Like how it might actually be quite difficult to talk about – To reconcile that place with this – Even to get up each morning, let alone *meet* people – No, it wasn't 'a laugh'. It was… It made me see that all of this is just a pretence stretched thin over pure… The purest nightmares.

SHERLOCK. I smoke, run noxious experiments, don't speak for days and I'm learning this.

SHERLOCK *threatens to play the violin.*

WATSON. I also smoke, hate silences and I'm determined to be a writer.

SHERLOCK. 'To be' as in 'trying' as in 'have nothing to write about in a market saturated with tacky war memoirs'. Apologies, you'll have to suffer the stairs again.

WATSON. I can observe a few things too.

SHERLOCK. I'm sure you can, Doctor –

WATSON. Self-destructive tendencies, wilful isolation, I'd say melancholy.

SHERLOCK. Is that a medical term?

WATSON. No, but judging by the state of your conversation, cripplingly awful melancholy.

SHERLOCK. You're doing it wrong.

WATSON. A dull, creeping thing that often comes with intelligence, a hollow, just here, where other people tell you 'joy' should be. So you think you're broken, hide it by being mean, consuming things to try and fill it, probably drink or (*Re. the toxins*) this stuff, maybe even other people – None of it works, just makes you feel like you're nothing but a bottomless appetite. Harm, with legs and a pulse. So it's easier, safer, to consider other people to be 'normals', 'dullards' – Push them away, pretend you've got control of the loneliness and give in to being empty – The problem you have is that it's not unique. We all struggle with it. All the time, all of us, and the only cure for it is other people and no, it wasn't during the retreat from Kandahar. It was Maiwand, trying to help my friend escape. 'Trying' as in 'failing'.

MRS HUDSON. Well, I'm glad to see you two are getting along.

SHERLOCK. Why write about it? If it's all just a pretence stretched over nightmares?

WATSON. I don't want to write about the wars –

SHERLOCK. You'd rather people lived on in blissful oblivion, how noble.

WATSON. I want to write something hopeful, something bigger –

SHERLOCK. Aaand it gets worse.

WATSON. *After* Afghanistan, I would do *anything* to give people that pretence.

SHERLOCK. Even lie to yourself?

WATSON. Even stay here and be civil to you, yes.

MRS HUDSON. Well, that settles it! I'll ask the driver to help with your things.

SHERLOCK *pursues* MRS HUDSON *out as 221B warps and melts…*

SHERLOCK. No, wait, Mrs Hudson.

MRS HUDSON. Do you know how many potentials you've already scared off?

SHERLOCK. But what if I just get a job and earn / a bit more…

MRS HUDSON. / You heard him, he's staying. What are you afraid of?

The world around SHERLOCK *grows misty and strange.*

SHERLOCK. Afraid – No, I'm just – Can it not be him, / pleeeease.

MRS HUDSON. / Sometimes only broken people can put each other back together again. You'll see.

SHERLOCK. No, but I don't think I actually want that –

MRS HUDSON. The battlefronts aren't only at the frontiers but everywhere, all the time.

SHERLOCK. Mrs Hudson?

The sounds of the jungle subsume the scene as MRS HUDSON *speaks with* MYCROFT*'s voice.*

MYCROFT (*voiceover*). / And the only thing keeping it all from collapse is the Big Show!

From the mists, SMALL *emerges, bleeding, terrifying and smiling.*

The performance of total control.

SHERLOCK. Private Small? What do you want? You're dead!

Animal cries build as SMALL *grabs* SHERLOCK *as if he has a desperate message to convey.*

MYCROFT (*voiceover*). British superiority – Militarily, organisationally, economically – is the biggest deterrent we have…

But when SMALL *makes to speak, instead of words, a tiny, brightly coloured frog hops from his mouth and into* SHERLOCK*'s hand.* SHERLOCK *panics.*

SHERLOCK. No, it's poison – Get it off me – Watson! Get it off –

SMALL *pushes* SHERLOCK *down and holds him in place as The Jade Dragon forms around him, complete with* BILL, LIN, MYCROFT *and* WATSON. POLICE *outside but nearby.*

WATSON!?

SMALL *is suddenly gone and* SHERLOCK *sits bolt upright, a syringe dangling from his bare chest.*

THE PRETENCE!

LIN (*Mandarin*). 點搞啊！他還活著 [*Diǎn gǎo a! tā hái huó zhe.*] [Holy crap, he's alive.]

SHERLOCK. It's about THE PRETENCE!

LIN. Calm, Mr Sherlock, you are in a / place of calm.

SHERLOCK. / Lin? Why are you doing a voice?

LIN (*in character*). As I said to your brother –

SHERLOCK. Mycroft? The poison, it's from arrow frogs –

MYCROFT. Licking frogs, Sherlock, even by your standards that's a new low –

SHERLOCK. Watson, you said you'd do anything so that people wouldn't have to face the nightmare of what the Empire is doing out there, the colonies, the –

WATSON. Holmes, it's a miracle you're alive.

SHERLOCK. Tonga is bringing that nightmare *here*. The cursed treasure, Amazonian blowguns – It's the Empire's worst fears! *They* tipped off the press – you were right, Watson – to *show* everyone the Top Secret Plans had been stolen and the police failing to retrieve them – To undermine the image of total control, expose the Big Show!

WATSON. So, the breakout –

SHERLOCK. From the fancy new jail – Exactly! All the cheap opium, the rumours about monsters – Fear, Watson! They're using Britain's fear!

WATSON. So Mary was set up to be the Sholto Murderess to –

SHERLOCK. – destabilise us, set us on each other and bring the Empire down from within!

Beat.

MYCROFT. Well, that's all I needed to hear. Glad I helped save your life, now back to prison.

WATSON. Mycroft, are you listening to this?

MYCROFT. Trying not to, unfortunately the nonsense tends to cut through – Can he walk?

WATSON. Walk!? He's lucky that poison wasn't fresh!

SHERLOCK. It wasn't fresh.

WATSON. Mycroft take me to Number Ten to get Mary's sentence commuted.

MYCROFT. Oh, my God, delusional – Constables, get in here!

BILL. I said no police.

MYCROFT. And I said yes police –

LIN (*Mandarin*). 糟糕, 要出大亂子了 [*Zāo gāo, yào chū dc luàn zi le.*] [Oh shit, this is gonna go pear-shaped.]

MYCROFT. Cuff them and take them back, please.

LIN. Bill, calm down.

SHERLOCK (*finally removing the syringe*). The zoo! Take me to the zoo!

MYCROFT. ENOUGH! You are BOTH going back into custody –

BILL. You lot, OUT!

A kerfuffle breaks out between BILL *and* POLICE.

SHERLOCK *throws one of them into* MYCROFT*, pulls down the curtains and sets about causing maximum chaos.*

SHERLOCK. FIIIIRE!! (*Encouraging him to shout.*) Watson – FIRE!

WATSON. Fire – FIRE!!

The fire might not catch but the chaos does! The call of 'Fire' repeats through The Jade Dragon as POLICE *struggle with* BILL *and* LIN. MYCROFT *flails wildly and* SHERLOCK *and* WATSON *run for it.*

SHERLOCK. Yes! Taxi, here!

SHERLOCK *jumps into a hansom cab.*

WATSON. What the HELL are you doing!?

SHERLOCK. Not sure, the only thing I know for sure's that I can't feel my hands and my tongue's gone weird.

DRIVER. Don't be sick in my cab, yeah?

SHERLOCK. Marylebone, fast as they'll go.

WATSON. Ah. Home, thank goodness. You rest, / I'll do what I can.

SHERLOCK. / Not home, the zoo! If only we'd lifted a list of the Wormwood Scrubs escapees from the station –

WATSON *supplies one.*

WATSON. Like this one?

SHERLOCK. Watson! You're getting better at this.

WATSON. And you're going home. (*To* DRIVER.) 221B Baker Street, no matter what he says.

SHERLOCK (*to* DRIVER). Ignore him, he's mad. The zoo! Watson, that poison only works when it's fresh. (*To* DRIVER.) And faster!

WATSON. You mean, Tonga's poison comes from –

SHERLOCK (*inspecting the list*). The zoo! And he's been filling London with animals from the colonies, a familiar kind of distraction, don't you think?

WATSON. So Tonga's at the zoo?

SHERLOCK. It's the last clue we have so – Are we – ? (*To* DRIVER.) Hey, why have we stopped?

DRIVER. Far as I'll go, mate.

SHERLOCK. What!? Why?

DRIVER. Regent's Park? This hour? Nah, there's something in there.

SHERLOCK (*leaving the cab*). Jesus Christ.

DRIVER. Neighbour told my mum a little girl had half her face bitten off –

SHERLOCK. Nothing moves faster around this city than gossip. / Pay the man for this too.

DRIVER. / Oi, what's he – ? That's mine! He's going straight for the park –

SHERLOCK *has taken the torch from the hansom cab and headed into the darkness of Regent's Park.*

WATSON. For God's sake…

WATSON *realises his personal effects are still at a police station.*

221B Baker Street, remember the address.

DRIVER. Oi!!

WATSON. Send the bill! Sorry, bye!

WATSON *rushes into the darkness as the cab disappears into the swirling fog of London at twilight…*

DRIVER. I knew it, you –

…we join SHERLOCK *in the mist of Regent's Park with the torch held aloft.* WATSON *catches up.*

WATSON (*breathless*). Holmes – Stop – That thorn was –

SHERLOCK. Gathering data, Watson –

WATSON. I know a suicide attempt when I see one.

SHERLOCK. Calm down.

WATSON. And killing yourself would be really – No, I need to say this –

SHERLOCK. We are being watched.

WATSON. SO!? You can't do that to –

SHERLOCK. I just don't mind the idea of no longer existing.

WATSON. What?

SHERLOCK. Quiet. We are being hunted.

WATSON. I mind.

SHERLOCK. No sudden moves. Whoever or whatever they are, they've concealed themselves. In the trees, perhaps. The zoo's this way.

WATSON *takes the torch from* SHERLOCK.

WATSON. But Holmes, not minding about –

SHERLOCK. Is now really the time?

WATSON. Now might be the only time – Look, even if you don't believe in the concept –

SHERLOCK (*noticing something on the ground*). Watson.

WATSON. I am / your friend.

SHERLOCK. / Your feet.

WATSON. What? (*Checking.*) Is this… blood?

The torchlight reveals a trail of blood leading to a tree, up the trunk, to a body draped over a branch, blood dripping to the floor.

After a moment, something pulls it out of sight and into the dark above.

SHERLOCK. Now might be a good moment for that revolver of yours.

WATSON. It would. If Lestrade hadn't taken it.

Something rustles in the trees.

The flame should ward them off. We'll be safe so long as we have this.

SHERLOCK. The enclosures, Watson. They're empty.

WATSON. What, the – the lions, bears, poisonous bloody –

SHERLOCK. All of them. You know what this means?

WATSON. We'll use the cages for shelter and talk there –

SHERLOCK. No, it means Tonga's done here –

WATSON. Then, there's no time –

SHERLOCK. This must be the final stage of his plan.

WATSON. Holmes, why do you think I write about you?

SHERLOCK. I need to concentrate –

WATSON. I write about you because you try.

SHERLOCK snatches WATSON's notepad and flips through it, reading moments aloud:

SHERLOCK. This is far bigger than you and your theories, you're a pistol in an artillery war –

WATSON. Despite everything –

SHERLOCK. This rebellion's everywhere.

WATSON. *Everything* you deduce about all of us.

SHERLOCK. In everyone. Even you.

WATSON. You're still here, trying –

SHERLOCK. He'd been servant to the Empress. They were shipping her off in secret –

WATSON. Trying to find the truth behind why we all do what we do.

SHERLOCK. It's the wealth of the Mughal dynasty! It once belonged to their last living heir – An Empress!

WATSON. So what does that mean about you, Sherlock?

The branches of the trees around them begin to shake.

SHERLOCK. Royal Engineers' tattoo. Explains how he blew open the safe.

WATSON. The cause of the melancholy is that despite the fact it's illogical, you do care.

SHERLOCK. Served in Sudan, likely the Balloon Section.

WATSON. That's the lie you're not facing.

SHERLOCK. There are only sixty names on the list of escapees.

WATSON. Did you hear anything I just said?

SHERLOCK. Sixty-one. Mycroft said sixty-one prisoners, there's sixty on the list – Which means there was one prisoner so secret, Mycroft didn't even admit she'd escaped –

WATSON. The death wish ends here.

SHERLOCK. The Empress, Watson! That's who Tonga was after all along.

WATSON. Holmes!

SHERLOCK. Watson!

Something heavy lands in the gloom beyond the torchlight and tumbles away.

WATSON. All this 'walking chemical reaction, heart is a muscle' bollocks, you're terrified!

SHERLOCK. Tonga is escaping with the Empress, the Secret Plans and the Treasure, they're leaving by air balloon –

WATSON. Terrified because you actually do care – I know you, Sherlock and it's killing you!

SHERLOCK. You're killing me! You are! This obsession with easy answers and narratives – Invented meaning – And when it came down to it, you chose the loved one –

SHERLOCK *is spooking the surrounding animals as he rages.*

WATSON. You were the loved one. I was trying to help *my best friend* –

SHERLOCK. For your books!

WATSON. No, cos I know what you'd do to yourself if you failed – and I can't lose another friend!

SHERLOCK. You're lying! Lying, Watson – *Friendship*!? You're cannibalising – You're a parasite using me for inspiration – You think I didn't read your book? I did, you changed everything about me – Made me into what you thought would advance your career – A calm little genius with safe little demons –

WATSON. No, Sherlock –

SHERLOCK. YOU DO NOT KNOW ME. The rebellions *in here,* that I am constantly – No, the last thing I want is to be by your side as it all burns – Stay away from me!

SHERLOCK *walks out into the darkness sending the animals wild and leaving* WATSON *with the torch.*

WATSON. Holmes, wait, at least take the… Holmes!?

WATSON *hears the animals screaming in the distance.*

SHERLOCK!?

WATSON *makes to leave but a tree ahead shakes.*

Alright, where is he going? To the air balloon or – ?

A branch breaks and something falls in the murk. WATSON *thrusts the torch flame around.*

Back! Stay back! Okay, alright, Tonga's escaping by balloon. Which means… He'd have to be way out in the countryside, away from buildings and prying eyes but he must've just been here to release all the – So he must be in London but clear of any buildings…

A branch shake and a screech takes his eyes up.

Yes, high up. Somewhere high and clear of buildings –

The torch is faltering and its pool of light constricting.

Don't go out. Not yet. Okay, if this was one of my stories, I would have seeded something early, picked it up conspicuously but not out of character later on…

The branches of the trees around start to shake with deadly predators and the torch is going out.

No, think, think! Gahd, this flame…

WATSON *empties his near-empty pockets.*

Must be something I can…

He considers lighting his notepad but decides to keep it.

No. Not yet. Um…

But then he discovers his box of matches.

Yes! But – (*Shakes the box out.*) Urgh, earwig infestation – Infestation! 'A snake infestation forced construction to a halt – '

He removes his hat, screws up the list of escapees and stuffs it into the hat as he speaks and then scrapes the sulphur from the ends of his Lucifer matches onto the paper in his hat.

At the circus, 'Always stay near the nest, snakes do – Won't go further'n a mile' but we're meant to believe they escaped the zoo and crawled through four miles of London to a building site!? Tonga took them there to shut it down, it's high, clear of other buildings – Yes! Tonga is at Tower Bridge!! Oh, God…

In the little remaining light he has from the torch, WATSON *is trying to light a sliver of torn paper as the* CREATURES *close in. Will it light or will they get to him first?!*

Come on…

He lights it! Suddenly, from out of the gloom, something runs at him and he drops the burning match into his hat.

A blast of flame momentarily illuminates the shapes of terrified animals and WATSON, *all running for their lives in murky, sweaty London…*

…our CHORUS *takes us through London in chaos, sweltering, riotous and wild – a whirl of characters new and old – brawls, looting, wide-spread rage – to arrive at…*

…Tower Bridge, a construction site, all metalwork and vertiginous danger!

PADSHAH BEGUM JAHAN *is illuminated by the treasure in the chest.* TONGA – *who, now that we know his real name, we will refer to as* AZAD – *is on the walkway:*

AZAD (*Hindustani*). Padshah Begum Jahaan!

BEGUM (*Hindustani*). *Azad! Aakhir tum aa gaye! Chalo, chalte hain!* [Azad! Finally! Let's go!]

AZAD (*Hindustani*). *Koi aa raha hai. Main usse rokta hoon – tum nikal jao!* [Someone's coming. I'll draw him away, whatever happens – you leave!]

BEGUM (*Hindustani*). *Main tumhare bina nahi jaaungi.* [Not without you.]

AZAD (*Hindustani*). *Bas khazana balloon tak le jao aur nikal jao!* [Just get the treasure onto the balloon and go!]

BEGUM (*Hindustani*). *Kya?* [What?]

AZAD (*Hindustani*). *Haan, khazana.* [Yes, the treasure.]

BEGUM (*Hindustani*). *Azad, yeh hamari amanat hai – hum saath karenge!* [Azad, this is our entrusted legacy – we do this together!]

SHERLOCK *arrives on the walkway between* AZAD *and where he wants to go. He is holding a flare – stolen from the police boat earlier – that he is prepared to set off. During the followng,* BEGUM *puts the treasure down and begins to pull in a large rope that extends off to something unseen.*

SHERLOCK. Tonga! It's over!

AZAD (*the faintest trace of his accent in the prologue*). That's not my name.

SHERLOCK. You tracked the treasure, murdered everyone who betrayed you and retrieved your Empress. But there's no way you're leaving Tower Bridge alive unless you surrender the Secret Plans and bring her in peacefully.

AZAD. Did you rehearse that?

SHERLOCK. The police will see this. (*Sets off the flare.*) If you don't do as I say –

AZAD. You're playing a role – You don't have to do any of this.

SHERLOCK. Like you didn't have to leave Arthur's body for me to find? What was that? A message? A trap?

AZAD. An invitation. You know what all of this is, that doesn't make your hands clean, you're part of it.

SHERLOCK. Everyone is!

AZAD. Then how do you explain me trying to help you? You don't have to be on the wrong side –

SHERLOCK. Stay back! The police will shoot you on sight!

AZAD. I made my peace with dying for this long ago.

SHERLOCK. You're only swapping one empire for another.

AZAD. This isn't an empire – We were invaded by a company. This isn't a country, it's a business with a flag and a national anthem. It's all run for the shareholders. Look how easily they turn on each other, they don't know who they are unless they're at war!

SHERLOCK. And you? Why is building that weapon so important to you?

AZAD. Because look how far talking is getting us.

AZAD heads to go past SHERLOCK – SHERLOCK ditches the flare – and shoves AZAD back.

SHERLOCK. Give up, Tonga.

AZAD. Don't call me that!

AZAD and SHERLOCK fight – a fight no one was prepared for – using whatever comes to hand.

SHERLOCK. You can't seriously expect to win against the British Empire.

AZAD. What matters is that we fight!

AZAD has SHERLOCK beaten. He's hanging off the walkway as per the ropes of a boxing ring.

WATSON (*off*). SHERLOCK!? Where are you!?

Having 'won', AZAD is heading back along the walkway towards the arch and his future! But, hearing WATSON, he rallies.

SHERLOCK (*spitting blood*). Watson! Stop the balloon!

Having heard SHERLOCK, AZAD stops and sees WATSON arrive at the base of the arch.

WATSON. What? Where is it?

SHERLOCK. Right bloody there!

The rope that BEGUM has been hauling in now reveals itself to be attached to a bloody hot air balloon!!

BEGUM (*Hindustani*). Sab taiyaar hai, Azad – chalo, jaldi! [Azad, it's ready – let's go!]

WATSON sees AZAD making for SHERLOCK and shouts a warning:

WATSON. Holmes, look out!

AZAD smashes SHERLOCK with something.

AZAD. You're too clever to die for this. Stay. Down.

AZAD heads off – WATSON heads up onto the arch as BEGUM heads for the treasure.

SHERLOCK gets up on the rails at the back, holds up a red envelope: The Top Secret Plans.

SHERLOCK. Azad? (*Spitting even more blood!*) That is your real name, isn't it?

AZAD checks inside his coat and retrieves his own red envelope, opens it:

AZAD (*reading*). 'Final Warning. Total rent in arrears… Love from Mrs Hudson.'

Of fucking course SHERLOCK lifted the plans during their fight!

BEGUM (*Hindustani*). *Hathiyar chhodo! Tum zyada zaroori ho! Chalo!* [You're more important than the weapon. Come with me and let's go, now!]

AZAD is torn.

WATSON. No. Stand fast, Tonga!

AZAD. Don't fucking call me that.

WATSON. Stand. Fast!

AZAD makes his decision – he rushes SHERLOCK for the letter.

SHERLOCK. Goodbye, Watson.

SHERLOCK grabs AZAD and they both fall over the edge of the walkway.

WATSON. SHERLOCK!!

BEGUM. Azad?

In a moment of deafening silence, we hear distant dogs barking and police whistles approaching.

BEGUM picks up the treasure and WATSON notices her.

WATSON. That… stuff.

BEGUM. It's been in my family for generations –

WATSON and BEGUM tussle over the treasure – WATSON hurts BEGUM and finds himself holding the chest and looking at the woman he has just harmed. He blames the treasure.

WATSON. It's bloody CURSED!

BEGUM. I'm taking it home.

WATSON. No. I'm gonna throw it in the Thames!

BEGUM. No!

WATSON tries to empty the treasure into the river far below. BEGUM wails on WATSON – he collapses onto the chest – refusing to let her near it.

Give it to me!

WATSON (*barking and growling like* SMALL). Get off it! It's got to go!

The POLICE *are getting nearer – whistles and sirens – BEGUM has to choose: treasure or freedom.*

BEGUM (*leaving*). No, there are people who need me.

She chooses freedom – gets into the balloon and makes her escape.

WATSON is dazed and bleeding – he tries to stand but crumples. BEGUM, heartbroken, makes her escape. WATSON is powerless to do anything with the rope trailing along behind her as she takes flight off, off, and then…

…SHERLOCK, bloodied and battered but miraculously alive, stumbles up onto the arch and grabs the rope.

SHERLOCK. Watson! The rope!

WATSON. Holmes? You're alive?

SHERLOCK. Of course I bloody am.

WATSON. How did you –

WATSON *slips and falls – he is clinging to the edge of Tower Bridge as* SHERLOCK *looks between him and the balloon.*

No, stop the balloon.

WATSON*'s hand slips – he is barely holding on –* SHERLOCK *makes his choice.*

SHERLOCK. No.

Instead of chasing the rope, SHERLOCK *pulls* WATSON *to safety.*

WATSON. Holmes, you idiot, you could have stopped her!

SHERLOCK. *I'm* the idiot, *you* shouldn't be here.

WATSON. You chose me.

SHERLOCK. How did you work out where I'd be?

WATSON. How did you survive?

SHERLOCK. At least she doesn't have the treasure or these Secret Plans.

WATSON. But how did you do that?

SHERLOCK. Bit like the rent money, luckily managed to goad the mastermind and get rid of him –

WATSON. But you can't have known you'd survive that fall.

SHERLOCK. She's almost out of range.

WATSON. Holmes, you can't do that –

SHERLOCK. POLICE! HERE!

WATSON (*losing it*). Holmes, listen! You can't do that to me! If it's the books, I won't write another word, you just can't – I can't take it, Sherlock, you can't do that –

SHERLOCK *hugs* WATSON *as whistles, barking dogs and* POLICE *flood the stage and we switch to...*

SHERLOCK. I'm sorry, John.

...221B Baker Street where MRS HUDSON *and* MARY *sit awkwardly together.*

MARY. Do you think Dr Watson will be long?

MRS HUDSON. Doubt it. How's it feel to be the richest woman in the Empire, eh? Richer than the Queen by the sounds of it.

MARY. Um…

MRS HUDSON. 'Spect you're mainly just glad you weren't hanged, eh?

MARY. Yes. And we both know who I have to thank for that.

MRS HUDSON. Still, nasty business.

MARY. In fact, they won't take any payment so I wondered if I might take care of their rent for the foreseeable future?

MRS HUDSON. Course, love! Be my guest. Here, do people recognise you? Out and about?

During the following, MRS HUDSON *retrieves a red envelope from nearby and hands it to* MARY. MARY *busies herself with it.*

MARY. Yep.

MRS HUDSON. Call you things?

MARY. Sometimes.

MRS HUDSON. Sholto Murderess? The Threat From Within!

MARY. Um –

MRS HUDSON. Nasty Rich Horrible Death Lady? D'you get that one?

MARY. Never before.

MRS HUDSON. And to think, you were innocent the whole time. It can't have been very nice for you. I got called all sorts *after* I murdered my husband.

MARY. Sorry?

From off, some banging and thumping, cursing and swearing. MARY *hands back a red envelope.*

WATSON *and* SHERLOCK *enter. Bruised but patched up, clean and recovered from their adventure.*

WATSON. All done, Mary!

MARY. Thank you, Doctor.

SHERLOCK. You'd best get it somewhere safe before the driver nicks off with the lot!

MARY. Right…

A pregnant moment between WATSON *and* MARY *that* SHERLOCK *does not comprehend.*

MRS HUDSON. Sherlock, how about we just nip out and keep an eye on it for her?

SHERLOCK. I was joking, we've paid an armed guard to watch it.

MRS HUDSON. Still, might be worth just nipping out –

SHERLOCK. I don't want to 'just nip out' –

MRS HUDSON. NOW!

MRS HUDSON *holds the door as she and* SHERLOCK *nip out.*

WATSON. Mary, I have something I want to ask –

MARY. Anything. You've saved my life, given me a future.

WATSON. Well, put you through something too –

MARY. That wasn't your doing.

WATSON. But you were in that terrible place and during that terrible breakout –

MARY. I had my Bible.

WATSON. Right, yeah, well… ahem.

WATSON *gets down on one knee.*

MARY. Oh, no, what's wrong?

WATSON. Nothing's wrong –

MARY. Is it your knee? The bullet?

WATSON. No, no, it's –

MARY. Let me help you – / You know lead poisoning can be –

WATSON. / No, Mary, it's – Just – Will you bloody marry me! …please. I couldn't actually afford a ring. This one's actually, well, its edible.

WATSON *produces a box with a Haribo-type ring inside.*

MARY. Oh, Dr Watson…

WATSON. John, please.

MARY. John… I'm sorry.

WATSON. No? Silly idea, I just – I thought, *after* all we'd been through, seize the day, you know.

MARY. That's why I'm leaving.

WATSON. Sorry?

MARY. I'm sure you'll understand that England doesn't feel so much like home any more. I've a tour planned. There's some Irish blood on my father's side, so I'll sail for Dublin first, then south and through that triumph of engineering the canal at Suez, Mother was from a small town on the River Nile so –

WATSON. When?

MARY. Well, I paid them to hold the boat for me –

WATSON. Right away?

MARY. There's lots to see. The Cape. Burma! My only hope is to find where I truly belong. Perhaps even to do some rea_, lasting good for those less fortunate than I've been.

WATSON. You're a good woman, Mary. The best.

MARY *kisses* WATSON *on the cheek.*

MARY. Thank you, John. Goodbye.

When MARY *leaves, she reveals* SHERLOCK *listening at the door. He tries to style it out.*

SHERLOCK. Yep. Bye, Mary.

MARY *leaves and* SHERLOCK *pretends not to see* WATSON *still on his knee.*

WATSON *eats the ring and then struggles to his feet.*

WATSON. I expect you heard that?

SHERLOCK. All of it. Very clearly, yes.

WATSON. Then you'll tell me it's all chemicals and nonsense feelings –

SHERLOCK. No. I know it hurts. Very much.

WATSON. Mind if I fire a few shots into the wall?

SHERLOCK. I'd prefer for you to write it into a story.

WATSON. Well, that might be the nicest thing you've *nearly* said to me.

SHERLOCK. Something hopeful, that helps people to see the details. Fiction, obviously.

WATSON. Obviously. No 'happy ever *after*s', hey?

SHERLOCK. Well, you could always rewrite that bit. She could say 'yes' at the end.

WATSON. As it happens… (*Retrieving a notepad.*) I did get to the end of the new one last night. /

SHERLOCK. / Oh God. /

WATSON. / Sketched out the last chapter, I mean, it's only a draft but – AHEM!

SHERLOCK. Aaaand he's gonna read aloud –

WATSON (*reading*).With the Secret Plans in safe hands and the

Mughal Treasure retrieved, Mycroft got to work. Mary had the noose about her neck when the stay of execution arrived. Soon *after*, the sensational appeal hearing took place, during which my friend Sherlock Holmes gave such a thoroughly comprehensive and indisputable account of events that all the charges against Mary were dropped.

SHERLOCK. Hm. Intricate and cleverly unfolded, Watson. Didn't Lestrade give evidence too?

WATSON. Yeah, but it wasn't very interesting.

SHERLOCK. Poor man, still trying to solve the Wormwood Scrubs breakout.

WATSON. I tried to tell him it was all Tonga, I mean Azad. But he said –

LESTRADE *steps into 221B Baker Street, a memory incarnate:*

LESTRADE. Nah, mate, you haven't seen the evidence. That breakout started on the inside.

LESTRADE *disappears into our* CHORUS, *who lurk at the edges of the scene.*

SHERLOCK. The *inside*?

WATSON. Yeah, since he's got his work cut out with those escapees, I thought it best not to mention the sixty-first. She's probably somewhere in India for all we know.

SHERLOCK. I opened the window.

WATSON. Sorry?

SHERLOCK. At Pondicherry Lodge, *after* I'd located the treasure.

As WATSON *checks his notepad, we see* MARY *swoon.* WATSON *drops his notepad to catch her. Throughout this section,* WATSON *and* SHERLOCK *interact with their memories:*

WATSON. She needs some air. Holmes! The window!

SHERLOCK *opens the window – he turns to see* THADDEUS.

MARY. Can't breathe –

WATSON. Outside. Holmes, the door!

SHERLOCK. Thaddeus, the authorities will be with you shortly. Thank you for the case.

THADDEUS *puts a hand to his neck, hit by a dart from a blowgun fired through the open window.*

The window had to be open for her plan to work.

AZAD *climbs through the open window as* WATSON *speaks.*

WATSON. Whose plan? Mary's? She was the one who insisted we call the authorities –

SHERLOCK. Because she knew Lestrade was overstretched.

LESTRADE *returns:*

LESTRADE. – last thing we need, what with the psycho in Whitechapel and rhinos in the parks –

SHERLOCK. She needed his suspicion.

A scream from off.

WATSON. Mary!

A form of Pondicherry Lodge arrives around them, THADDEUS *is dead, sat in a chair facing away from the window. His face contorted into a smiling grimace.* MARY *clutching her Bible, staring.*

Mary? Are you okay?

LESTRADE. Is his face normally like that?

SHERLOCK. She already had Arthur's file, she just needed to get arrested.

MARY. The curse.

ALL. The cuuuuurse.

WATSON. You mean, the building projects, the map of –

Our CHORUS *folds a large set of blueprints into* MARY*'s Bible.*

SHERLOCK. Of Wormwood Scrubs, yes. She led the breakout from the inside.

MARY sets her Bible down as WATSON *speaks as we recreate a glimpse of the courthouse:*

WATSON. This is Mary we're talking about! How could she possibly have smuggled those blueprints into…

MARY. / They wouldn't even let me take my Bible –

WATSON (*grabbing the Bible from* LESTRADE). For God's sake, man! Show a little… (*In 221B again.*) Ooooh, sugar. But she didn't leave with the breakout, she stayed in her cell when she was sentenced to death, why risk that?

AZAD. I made my peace with dying for this long ago.

SHERLOCK. They needed the Empress, everyone else was disposable.

AZAD. What matters is that we fight.

WATSON. But the balloon? How could they possibly have –

Ding-ding! SHERLOCK *places a paper in* WATSON*'s hand. We're back at the boxing for a moment:*

(*Reading.*) 'The Royal Engineers have lost a military air balloon – '

SHERLOCK. Domingo was ex-Royal Engineers.

WATSON. But, Holmes, the expense and planning – ?

A cab forms around SHERLOCK, WATSON *and* MARY

SHERLOCK. If you've received three gifts like this, why still work as a governess?

MARY. How did you know?

WATSON. She dodged the question. She used those gifts to set the plan in motion.

MARY. Milk stain on sleeve.

SHERLOCK. The clues were too obvious.

MARY. Grass stains at just the height of a child's foot when carried.

SHERLOCK – *pursued by* WATSON – *steps out of the four-wheeler and back into 221B Baker Street.*

SHERLOCK. Mary Morstan wrote herself like a story for us to read.

MARY. Perhaps those books of yours are working *after* all, Doctor!

WATSON. It's not Mary Morstan. She didn't take her father's name.

AZAD. An invitation.

WATSON. He'd disowned her, let her mother die in poverty –

AZAD. You don't have to be on the wrong side.

DOMINGO. This rebellion's everywhere. In everyone. Even you.

SHERLOCK. All of this was about lighting the touch paper. Who knows how many cells and splinter cells she could have inspired!?

WATSON. So… the woman I fell for – Who I just proposed to… was a –

MARY. – fiction.

WATSON. In fact, she was trying to start –

MARY. A Revolution.

A flash briefly illuminates our CHORUS – *ready for battle –* MARY *leading them as a pulse begins.*

WATSON. And Holmes… We just loaded all that treasure into
her taxi! She's going to Ireland, Egypt, India – the Empress!?
Think what she could do with it all.

As WATSON *gets ready,* SHERLOCK *retrieves the red
envelope and opens it.*

It's lucky you've been lording it over your brother with those
Secret Plans otherwise she'd have all she needs for a full-
scale war.

SHERLOCK *closes the envelope. Gulp.*

I mean this is… *brilliant,* isn't it? Brilliant! Cos you know
what this means? We've found you a nemesis for the next
book! Quickly then… Holmes?

SHERLOCK. I just… I don't know what's right.

WATSON. Look… The way I see it, this age of empires, it's a
phase. Beyond this, there is a more equal, fairer world. But
the only way out is through. And I have something that Mary
doesn't have. A publishing deal. Sherlock, you are our secret
weapon.

SHERLOCK. I'm your… what?

WATSON. A detective, anti-establishment, a people's hero – It's
like Mycroft said, we've got the story for the Big Show!
Now, we just need to stop her so we get the right ending.

SHERLOCK. What about your stick?

WATSON. I'll be fine without it. Need to be able to take notes.
Let's go!

SHERLOCK. Watson… what actually is Mary's surname?

For the first time in our play, SHERLOCK *becomes properly
aware of the* CHORUS *around him.*

WATSON. Oh, she took the surname of the Irish nanny who
raised her. It's –

SHERLOCK. Moriarty.

WATSON *holds the door open for* SHERLOCK *to leave through.*

WATSON. Are you coming or not?

SHERLOCK....

The pulsing explodes into the rhythm of a dance. The dance we've been building to throughout. A dance of rebellion, rage and hope.

The End.

Established in 1932, the multi-award-winning Regent's Park Open Air Theatre is one of the largest theatres in London (at a capacity of 1,304). Passionate about producing popular, enriching and unexpected theatre that provides a lens into the here and now, the scale and ambition of our productions together with our magical outdoor setting, makes us unique in the capital's cultural landscape.

Led by Joint Chief Executives Drew McOnie (Artistic Director) and James Pidgeon (Executive Director), we welcome over 175,000 visitors to our summer season every year. Our productions also continue to tour the UK and internationally reaching a live audience of just under 1 million people worldwide in 2025 alone.

As a registered charity that receives no regular public subsidy, we rely entirely on earned income and charitable contributions. Nevertheless, we offer £15 tickets across the whole of our summer season, and we regularly work with a range of local charities. Each year, on average, we subsidise tickets for 6,000 school pupils.

Regent's Park Open Air Theatre has become one of the most independently sustainable and financially successful producing theatres in the country, and we're proud to embark on the next stage of our vision with ever-increasing artistic ambition and entrepreneurial spirit.

openairtheatre.com

Martin Sebaldt

Die Institutionen der Bundesrepublik Deutschland in der Ordnung des Grundgesetzes

Die Institutionen der Bundesrepublik
Deutschland in der Ordnung des
Grundgesetzes

Martin Sebaldt

Die Institutionen der Bundesrepublik Deutschland in der Ordnung des Grundgesetzes

Konstanz und Wandel im Überblick

Inhalt

1. Einführung

Das 1949 verabschiedete Grundgesetz ist die verfassungsrechtliche Basis der politischen Ordnung Deutschlands. Es legt die Funktionen und Kompetenzen der Verfassungsorgane fest, bestimmt deren Beziehungen zueinander und regelt auch den Austrag und die Schlichtung von Streitigkeiten.

Darüber hinaus finden sich im Grundgesetz detaillierte Bestimmungen zum Gang der Gesetzgebung sowie zur Kompetenzabgrenzung zwischen Bund und Ländern, die in einer föderalen politischen Ordnung unabdingbar sind. Jüngeren Datums sind schließlich noch Normen, welche das Verhältnis Deutschlands zur Europäischen Union regeln.

Die vorliegende kleine Schrift dient der Schaffung systematischen Wissens über die Institutionenordnung des Grundgesetzes. Sie fußt auf meinem Text für die Lerneinheit „Die Institutionen der Bundesrepublik Deutschland im Kontext der Verfassungsordnung des Grundgesetzes" des Lehrprojekts „Politikwissenschaft online" (PolitikON).

Da dieses Internet-Portal der Deutschen Vereinigung für Politische Wissenschaft (DVPW) inzwischen dauerhaft abgeschaltet ist, mache ich diesen Text hiermit in einer Neufassung wieder zugänglich. Folgende Einzelfragen sollen dabei beantwortet werden:

1. Was fällt im Einzelnen unter den Begriff „Verfassung", und wie stellt sich die bundesdeutsche Verfassungsordnung im Überblick dar?

2. Welche Verfassungstraditionen gibt es, die Geist und Inhalt des Grundgesetzes maßgeblich beeinflusst haben?
3. Wie ist das Grundgesetz formal aufgebaut, und welche Prinzipien und Staatsziele, die auch die Funktionsweise der einzelnen Institutionen vorprägen, sind dort im Einzelnen verankert?
4. Welche Vorgaben macht unsere Verfassung zu Stellung, Aufbau und Funktionen dieser Institutionen?
5. Wie sind die Beziehungen zwischen ihnen verfassungsrechtlich vorgeprägt und geregelt?
6. Welche Änderungen hat unser Grundgesetz seit 1949 erfahren, die auch das Verhältnis zwischen den Institutionen modifiziert haben?
7. Welche wesentlichen Entwicklungen sind in der Verfassungspraxis seit 1949 zu beobachten, und wie werden diese von der Forschung bewertet?

Auf einen Anmerkungsapparat wurde aus Gründen der Übersichtlichkeit verzichtet. Jedoch finden sich in der Bibliographie zentrale Studien zu den einzelnen Themenschwerpunkten.

2. Grundlagen

Die Verfassungsordnung des Grundgesetzes definiert den Handlungsrahmen der einzelnen politischen Institutionen Deutschlands. Konkret umfasst sie alle Normen, welche diese erst ins Leben rufen, ihre Kompetenzen definieren und ihre Aufgabenfelder von denjenigen anderer Institutionen abgrenzen. Im Folgenden soll ein Überblick über die einzelnen Elemente von Verfassungsordnungen gegeben werden, die diese Aufgaben erfüllen.

2.1 Der Begriff der Verfassung

Der Begriff der Verfassung ist nicht einheitlich definiert. Im weiteren Sine meint er „die Gesamtheit derjenigen Regeln und Strukturen, die das Gemeinwesen und damit die politische Ordnung prägen" (Hans Fenske). Im engeren Sinne meint er eine einheitliche, geschriebene Verfassung, also ein Verfassungsdokument 'aus einem Guss', wie etwa die Verfassung der USA von 1787 oder eben auch das deutsche Grundgesetz von 1949.

Folgt man der weiter gehaltenen Definition, versteht man aber unter „Verfassung" nicht nur diese Verfassungsurkunden, sondern auch alle übrigen Normen, welche die Struktur eines politischen Systems prägen. Im Einzelnen sind dies:

- Schlüsselgesetze mit einem verfassungsäquivalenten Charakter;
- Einfache Gesetze und abgeleitete Normen;
- Richterrecht;
- Gewohnheitsrecht;
- Konventionen.

Bevor im nächsten Schritt die deutschen Verhältnisse in den Blick genommen werden, sei dieser Sachverhalt an Beispielen anderer Systeme schlaglichtartig illustriert, welche die praktische Bedeutung dieser übrigen Normentypen für die Funktionsfähigkeit politischer Ordnungen belegen.

- Es gab und gibt Systeme, die über keine einheitliche geschriebene Verfassungsurkunde verfügen. Großbritannien, Neuseeland und Israel kommen ohne ein derartiges Dokument aus, und auch die französische Dritte Republik (1870/75-1940) verfügte darüber nicht. Stattdessen gründen solche Ordnungen im Kern auf einer Reihe von *Einzelgesetzen*, welche *Verfassungsqualität* besitzen und zusammengenommen ein Äquivalent für eine einheitliche Verfassungsurkunde bilden.

  In Großbritannien sind dies u.a. die Habeas Corpus Akte von 1679, die Bill of Rights von 1689 und die Parliament Acts von 1911 und 1949, die der Garantie der Grundrechte, der Verankerung der Parlamentssouveränität und

der Vorherrschaft des demokratisch gewählten
Unterhauses gegenüber dem Oberhaus dienen.

- Auch *einfache Gesetze* können die politische Institutionenordnung maßgeblich bestimmen. So etwa haben die Wahlrechtsreformen der Jahre 1832, 1867, 1884/85 und 1918/28 maßgeblich zur Demokratisierung des britischen politischen Systems beigetragen und damit die Natur und die Zusammensetzung des Parlaments entscheidend verändert: Erst durch die Einführung des allgemeinen Wahlrechts konnte es der Arbeiterbewegung in Form der Labour Party gelingen, in das Unterhaus einzuziehen und die Machtverhältnisse dort maßgeblich zu verändern.

- *Richterrecht*, insbesondere höchstrichterliche Entscheidungen, können zur Prägung des Institutionengefüges ebenfalls maßgeblich beitragen. So ist das heute unbestrittene Normenkontrollrecht des Obersten Gerichtshofs der USA (Supreme Court) in der Verfassungsurkunde gar nicht verankert: Im Rahmen eines Urteils (Marbury vs. Madison) nahm der Supreme Court im Jahre 1803 ein solches 'Recht' einfach in Anspruch, indem er im angesprochenen Fall ein Gesetz für verfassungswidrig erklärte. Da dieser Akt unwidersprochen blieb, bekam er Präzedenzcharakter und etablierte somit qua Tradition das bis heute bestehende gerichtliche Normenkontrollrecht, welches den gesetzgeberischen Spielraum von Kongress und Präsident nicht unwesentlich eingeschränkt hat.

- Auch *ungeschriebenes Gewohnheitsrecht* trägt zur Prägung des Institutionengefüges bei. So ist im britischen „Common Law" seit Urzeiten, obwohl später auch gesetzlich bekräftigt, das Prinzip des fairen und regelgeleiteten Rechtsverfahrens („by due process of law") verankert. Es schützt das Individuum bis heute gegen staatliche Willkürentscheidungen und irregulär ablaufende Prozesse, war aber auch strukturbildend für den politischen Entscheidungsprozess. Denn dass parlamentarische Debatten und Beschlüsse nach präzisen und einheitlichen Regeln abzulaufen haben, entspringt ebenfalls dieser gewohnheitsrechtlichen Tradition, was an der bis heute ritualisierten britischen Debattenpraxis besonders gut abzulesen ist.

- Schließlich können auch *Verfassungskonventionen* („constitutional conventions") eine bedeutende Rolle spielen. Bis heute etwa steht nirgends geschrieben, dass der britische Premierminister obligatorisch dem Unterhaus angehören müsse. Gleichwohl hat sich das per Tradition seit dem frühen 20. Jahrhundert 'eingebürgert' und gilt als allgemein akzeptierte Konvention über die Parteigrenzen hinweg: Derlei „constitutional conventions" unterliegen zwar durch ihren informellen Charakter starken Wandlungen, was ihre generelle Bedeutung jedoch nicht schmälert.

2.2 Die Verfassungsordnung Deutschlands

Auch in Deutschland spielen diese unterschiedlichen Normentypen für die Prägung des Institutionengefüges eine große Rolle, wobei jedoch das Gewicht geschriebenen Rechts signifikant höher ist als im angloamerikanischen Raum. Neben dem Grundgesetz, das als Verfassungsurkunde natürlich eine dominierende Funktion innehat und später noch genauer auf seinen institutionenprägenden Charakter analysiert wird, sind jedoch auch die übrigen Elemente einer Verfassungsordnung vorfindbar. Aufgrund ihrer Masse kann deren Bedeutung an dieser Stelle aber nur schlaglichtartig beleuchtet werden.

- *Einfache Gesetze* mit *institutionenprägendem Charakter* spielen in der Bundesrepublik eine große Rolle und konkretisieren das Grundgesetz dort, wo es gewollt oder ungewollt keine genaueren Vorgaben macht. So finden sich im *Gesetz über das Bundesverfassungsgericht* detaillierte Vorgaben zur Organisation des obersten deutschen Gerichts, zur notwendigen Qualifikation der Richter und zum genauen Wahlverfahren ebenso wie zu den einzelnen Verfahrensarten. Damit hat dieses Einzelgesetz Zusammensetzung, Selbstverständnis und Arbeitsweise des Bundesverfassungsgerichts wesentlich mehr geprägt als das Grundgesetz selbst, das hierzu nur allgemeine Vorgaben macht.

- Gleiches gilt für das *Bundeswahlgesetz*, das nicht nur die prozeduralen Einzelheiten der Wahlen zum Deutschen Bundestag festlegt, sondern auch das gesamte Wahlsystem als personalisierte Verhältniswahl erst verankert. Denn im Grundgesetz ist in Artikel 38 nur der Grundsatz allgemeiner, unmittelbarer, freier, gleicher und geheimer Wahl festgeschrieben sowie das aktive Mindestwahlalter von 18 Jahren.

  Alles Übrige wird der einzelgesetzlichen Regelung übertragen, durch welche auch die Zusammensetzung des Bundestages und die Struktur des deutschen Parteiensystems maßgeblich geprägt wurden. Denn nicht zuletzt der Grundsatzentscheidung für ein modifiziertes Verhältniswahlrecht ist es zuzuschreiben, dass Kleinparteien in den Bundestag gelangen, absolute Mehrheiten einzelner Parteien verhindern und im Regelfall Koalitionen aus mehreren Fraktionen erzwingen konnten.

- Eine ähnlich bedeutende Rolle spielt schließlich auch das *Parteiengesetz*, das nicht nur den Funktionskatalog bundesdeutscher Parteien präzise definiert, sondern auch genaue Vorgaben zur innerparteilichen Organisation und insbesondere zur Gewährleistung innerparteilicher Demokratie macht. Verhindert werden soll somit das Erstarken antidemokratischer Parteien, und zusätzlich sollen präzise rechtliche Grundlagen für etwaige Parteiverbote geschaffen werden.

Denn wenn eine Partei sowohl dem Grundsatz innerparteilicher Demokratie nicht genügen als auch die politische Ordnung des Grundgesetzes ablehnen sollte, existieren nunmehr konkrete Normen für ein Verbotsverfahren vor dem Bundesverfassungsgericht. Darüber hinaus sind hier die detaillierten und immer wieder kontrovers diskutierten Regeln zur Finanzierung der Parteien festgeschrieben, die bei einem Verstoß empfindliche Strafen für die betroffenen Organisationen nach sich ziehen können.

- Nicht nur Gesetze, sondern auch *Geschäftsordnungen* der einzelnen Institutionen können diese Konkretisierungsfunktion übernehmen. So haben sich die meisten unserer Verfassungsorgane (Bundestag, Bundesrat, Bundesregierung, Bundesverfassungsgericht) selbst solche Ordnungen gegeben, um ihren Arbeitsablauf im Einzelnen zu organisieren, was für die politische Praxis von großer Bedeutung ist. So macht etwa die *Geschäftsordnung des Deutschen Bundestages* (GOBT) detaillierte Vorgaben zum Ablauf der Debatten und zur Organisation von Fraktionen und Ausschüssen.

Dort ist z.B. festgeschrieben, dass Tagesordnung und Rednerabfolge im Ältestenrat parteiübergreifend im Konsens geregelt werden, was für die Debattenkultur prägend wurde und trotz parteipolitischer Kontrovesen im Bundestag ein kooperatives Arbeitsklima auch zwischen Regierung und Opposition gefördert hat – keineswegs selbstverständlich, wenn wir an die kompetitivere Szenerie des britischen Unterhauses denken.

- *Richterrecht* spielt in Deutschland vor allen Dingen in der Form verfassungsgerichtlicher Entscheidungen eine große Rolle. Im Unterschied zu den USA ist das Normenkontrollrecht des Bundesverfassungsgerichts schon im Grundgesetz explizit verankert. Dies hat zu einer langen Reihe entsprechender Verfahren geführt, die das bundesdeutsche Institutionensystem nachhaltig beeinflusst haben. Gleiches gilt für die Organ- und die Bund-Länderstreitverfahren, in welchen die einzelnen Verfassungsorgane gegeneinander bzw. Bundesländer gegenüber ihnen klagebefugt sind, wenn sie ihre Rechte verletzt sehen.

Am Beispiel des 'Blauhelmurteils' von 1994 sei die Bedeutung solcher Richtersprüche illustriert: Die Beteiligung deutscher Militärkontingente an UN-Friedensmissionen außerhalb des NATO-Bündnisgebiets, die die Bundesregierung ohne parlamentarische Zustimmung verfügt hatte, sollte durch eine Klage der SPD-Bundestagsfraktion vor dem Bundesverfassungsgericht für verfassungswidrig erklärt werden, da sie dem Verfassungsgebot, Streitkräfte nur zu Verteidigungszwecken einzusetzen, widerspräche.

Die Verfassungsrichter lehnten diese Auffassung unter Verweis auf den Friedensmissionscharakter der Operationen unter Federführung der UNO ab, deren Teilnahme das Grundgesetz erlaube. Es machte aber der Bundesregierung gleichzeitig künftig zur Pflicht, eine derartige

Entscheidung durch einen entsprechenden Bundestagsbeschluss bestätigen zu lassen. Die sicherheitspolitische Kooperationspraxis zwischen Bundestag und Bundesregierung hat dieses Urteil somit entscheidend beeinflusst.

- Die Bedeutung von *Gewohnheitsrecht* und *Konventionen* ist in der bundesdeutschen Rechtsordnung von geringerer Bedeutung als in anderen Staaten, zumal der Spielraum hierfür durch die stetig voranschreitende Verrechtlichung kontinuierlich geschwunden ist. Gleichwohl können die einzelnen Institutionen ohne informellen 'Korpsgeist', der eben nur per Konvention entstehen kann, nicht bestehen. So ist es Tradition, bei krankheitsbedingter Abwesenheit von Abgeordneten ein sog. „pairing" durchzuführen: dann bleiben von den nicht betroffenen Fraktionen ebenfalls so viele Parlamentarier der Abstimmung fern, dass der parteipolitische Proporz wieder hergestellt ist.

Auch ist es gute Sitte, einen neuen Abgeordneten nach seiner 'Jungfernrede' parteien- und lagerübergreifend mit wohlwollendem Beifall zu bedienen, um ihn quasi offiziell in der Gemeinschaft der Parlamentarier willkommen zu heißen. Und schließlich ist auch der zweckorientierte und in der Regel kooperative Arbeitsstil in den Ausschüssen nicht durch Geschäftsordnungen erzwingbar, sondern muss sich aus dem Abgeordnetenselbstverständnis erst entwickeln.

3. Vorgeschichte und Entstehung des Grundgesetzes

Die Tradition geschriebener Verfassungen, die auch Struktur und Inhalt des Grundgesetzes maßgeblich beeinflusst hat, reicht in Deutschland bis in das frühe 19. Jahrhundert zurück. Französischen Vorbildern (Revolutionsverfassung von 1791, Charte von 1814) folgend und geistesgeschichtliche Modelle von Rationalismus, Aufklärung und Liberalismus rezipierend, setzte sich der Trend immer mehr durch, das Gefüge eines politischen Systems durch eine einheitliche grundgesetzliche Basis zu formen und die Kompetenzen der einzelnen politischen Institutionen präzise zu definieren. Im Folgenden sollen diejenigen Traditionsbestände in Deutschland genauer unter die Lupe genommen werden, welche die Architektur unseres Grundgesetzes entscheidend vorgeprägt haben.

3.1 Deutsche Verfassungstraditionen des 19. Jahrhunderts

Nach dem Zerfall des Heiligen Römischen Reiches Deutscher Nation und nach dem Ende der napoleonischen Kriege waren die deutschen Fürsten zwar bestrebt, die alten monarchischen Ordnungen wiederzubeleben. Jedoch hatte sich gerade der Gedanke einer Grundlegung staatlicher Ordnung durch eine moderne geschriebene Verfassung schon so weit verbreitet, dass er auch im Deutschland des

19. Jahrhunderts nicht mehr souverän missachtet werden konnte.

Bereits die 1815 verabschiedete Akte des neu konstituierten Deutschen Bundes schrieb den Mitgliedern in Artikel 13 die Schaffung „landständischer" Verfassungen vor. Und auch wenn längst nicht alle dieser Vorgabe nachkamen und insbesondere die dominierenden Mächte Preußen und Österreich sie jahrzehntelang ignorierten, begann sich vor allen Dingen in den süddeutschen Staaten eine Verfassungstradition zu entwickeln, die ganz erkennbar von liberalem Gedankengut geprägt war: Bayern und Baden gaben sich bereits im Jahr 1318 eigene Verfassungen und wurden damit zu Wegbereitern der späteren Konstitutionalisierung Gesamtdeutschlands.

Aber auch der Deutsche Bund selbst blieb diesbezüglich nicht ohne Einfluss, verankerte er doch das bis heute in Deutschland geltende *Bundesratsprinzip* in seiner Akte: Eine parlamentarische Kammer auf Bundesebene, welche der Vertretung von Länderinteressen dienen soll, besteht diesem zufolge nicht aus gewählten unabhängigen Abgeordneten (Senatsprinzip), sondern aus weisungsabhängigen Delegierten der Landesregierungen. Diesem Prinzip gemäß setzte sich die „Bundesversammlung" des Deutschen Bundes zusammen, und auch die meisten späteren gesamtdeutschen Verfassungen (Reichsverfassung von 1871, Weimarer Verfassung von 1919) blieben diesem Grundsatz treu. Das implizierte zudem eine Grundsatzentscheidung für eine *föderalistische* politische Ordnung: Vom zentralistischen Dritten Reich einmal abgesehen beruht die deutsche Verfassungstradition auf dem Prinzip der *Bundesstaatlichkeit*; einheitsstaatliche Visionen spielten keine maßgebliche Rolle.

Freilich waren die deutschen politischen Systeme des 19. Jahrhunderts durchweg noch *Obrigkeitsstaaten*, in denen das Prinzip monarchischer Souveränität auch nach der Schaffung von Verfassungen noch galt: Die Parlamente waren in ihren Kompetenzen eingeschränkt, besaßen vielfach nicht einmal ein eigenes Gesetzesinitiativrecht und waren auch in ihren Legislativbefugnissen durch ein absolutes königliches Vetorecht behindert. Die politische Verantwortlichkeit der Minister vor den Volksvertretungen existierte meist ebenfalls noch nicht; Kabinettsmitglieder waren zunächst nur dem monarchischen Souverän rechenschaftspflichtig. Lediglich die Paulskirchenverfassung von 1849, die aber nie Gültigkeit erlangte, setzte schon deutlich demokratischere Akzente, indem sie die vollständige gesetzgeberische Gleichberechtigung des zweikammerigen Reichstags festschrieb.

Immerhin etablierte diese Verfassungstradition das bis heute geltende Prinzip, die Kompetenzen der einzelnen politischen Institutionen genau festzuschreiben und auch ihre Beziehungen untereinander festzulegen. Diese Bestimmungen bildeten dann jeweils auch den Ausgangspunkt für den Kampf um die Ausweitung eigener Macht, der insbesondere von den Parlamenten hartnäckig und letztlich erfolgreich geführt wurde: Durch formelle Verfassungsänderungen bzw. durch Wandel der

Verfassungspraxis gestanden die monarchischen Souveräne nun auch das parlamentarische Initiativrecht für Gesetzesvorlagen zu sowie die Einflussnahme auf die Zusammensetzung der jeweiligen Regierungen.

Die Reichsverfassung von 1871 verankerte das Gesetzesinitiativrecht des demokratisch gewählten Reichstages bereits explizit, verweigerte jedoch formell noch die Verantwortlichkeit des Reichskanzlers und seiner Staatssekretäre vor den Parlamentariern, die nach wie vor nur dem Kaiser rechenschaftspflichtig waren und nur von ihm ernannt und entlassen werden konnten. Und doch war die preußisch dominierte Reichsleitung zu einer immer stärkeren Kooperation mit den Parlamentariern gezwungen, um für großangelegte Gesetzgebungsprojekte (Sozialversicherung, Kulturkampf- und Sozialistengesetze etc.) sichere Mehrheiten zu finden, und berücksichtigte dies zunehmend bei der Auswahl der Regierungsmitglieder: Geschick im Umgang mit dem Reichstag wurde als 'Berufungskriterium' nun immer wichtiger.

Eine schleichende Parlamentarisierung des wilhelminischen Kaiserreichs war somit in die Wege gesetzt, die durch den Ersten Weltkrieg noch erheblich beschleunigt wurde: Auflegung und Billigung umfangreicher Kriegskredite banden Reichsleitung und Reichstag noch enger aneinander, und als im Jahre 1918 die deutsche Niederlage absehbar und das Scheitern der kaiserlichen Politik augenscheinlich geworden war, rang man sich noch im Oktober kurz vor der Revolution zu einer Verfassungsrevision durch, die nun auch die formelle Abhängigkeit der Regierung vom parlamentarischen Vertrauen festschrieb. Durch den Sturz des Hauses Hohenzollern und die Ausrufung der Republik erlangten diese Änderungen jedoch keine praktische Bedeutung mehr.

3.2 Die Weimarer Reichsverfassung als Lernobjekt

Die Architekten der Weimarer Verfassung schlossen eng an diese Verfassungstradition an: Sie verankerten nunmehr auch formell das parlamentarische Prinzip und schrieben zudem die bundesstaatliche Tradition fort: Der Reichskanzler und die einzelnen Reichsminister wurden zwar nach wie vor nicht vom Reichstag gewählt, sondern vom Reichspräsidenten ernannt und auch entlassen. Nunmehr jedoch konnte jedes Regierungsmitglied durch ein parlamentarisches Misstrauensvotum zum Rücktritt gezwungen werden.

Der nach dem Bundesratsprinzip zusammengesetzte Reichsrat war als parlamentarische Ländervertretung obligatorisch an der Reichsgesetzgebung beteiligt, verfügte aber im Konfliktfall gegenüber dem Reichstag nur über ein suspensives Vetorecht: Einsprüche der Länderkammer gegen Beschlüsse des Reichstags konnten von ihm überstimmt werden, was die Macht des Reichsrates erheblich beschränkte und der bundesstaatlichen Ordnung der

Weimarer Republik einen viel *unitarischeren* Charakter verlieh als der heutigen Bundesrepublik.

Auch ein „Staatsgerichtshof für das Deutsche Reich" zur Schlichtung von Kompetenzstreitigkeiten zwischen und innerhalb von einzelnen Ländern sowie von Konflikten zwischen dem Reich und den Gliedstaaten fand nun Eingang in die Verfassung, was das gewachsene Gewicht verfassungsgerichtlicher Tradition insbesondere in den USA reflektiert. Jedoch besaß dieses Reichsgericht noch nicht das Normenkontrollrecht und auch nicht die Kompetenz zur Regelung von Konflikten zwischen den Reichsorganen. Die Überprüfung einzelner Gesetzesvorlagen auf ihre Verfassungskonformität lag damit letztlich bei den Parlamentariern selbst, nicht bei den Richtern. Und doch kann dieses Reichsgericht als Vorstufe für die Schaffung eines vollwertigen Verfassungsgerichts gewertet werden, die im Grundgesetz durch das Bundesverfassungsgericht schließlich gelang.

Dass die Verfassungsordnung der Weimarer Republik am Ende scheiterte, kann letztlich nicht ihr selbst zum Vorwurf gemacht werden, sondern den politischen Rahmenbedingungen: Zwar trugen die ausgeprägten Notverordnungsrechte des Reichspräsidenten im Artikel 48 der Verfassung zum Kollaps des Systems bei, indem sie Hindenburg das Regieren mit parlamentarisch nicht verantwortlichen Kabinetten ermöglichten.

Im Kern jedoch etablierte die Weimarer Verfassung ein 'ganz normales' parlamentarisches Regierungssystem – allerdings mit ausgeprägten Präsidialbefugnissen –, das im Rahmen einer demokratischen politischen Kultur und eines stabilen Parteiensystems wohl gut funktioniert hätte. Da jedoch im Deutschland der zwanziger und frühen dreißiger Jahre weder das eine noch das andere existierte, sondern ein Staatsgefüge ohne stabilen demokratischen Konsens, war die Weimarer Ordnung trotzdem zum Scheitern verurteilt.

3.3 Die Alliierten: Verfassungspläne der Sieger

Die Institutionenordnung des Grundgesetzes wurde nach dem Ende des Zweiten Weltkriegs zum einen durch die Pläne der alliierten Siegermächte maßgeblich beeinflusst. Von der Sowjetunion einmal abgesehen, die letztlich die Schaffung eines neuen Satellitenstaates mit sozialistischer 'Verfassungsordnung' anstrebte, bestand Grundkonsens bezüglich der Schaffung einer neuen demokratischen Verfassung.

Bereits vor 1949 waren in den vier Besatzungszonen die Länder durch eigene Verfassungen wieder entstanden bzw. als Neuschöpfungen konstituiert worden. Die in den westlichen Zonen nach alliierter Billigung mehrheitlich verankerten *parlamentarischen Regierungssysteme* hatten insoweit Einfluss auf die Schaffung des Grundgesetzes, als die USA, Großbritannien und Frankreich die Schaffung einer derartigen parlamentarischen Verfassungsordnung im Unterschied zu einem Präsidialsystem nun auch auf Bundesebene präferierten.

Weniger Einigkeit bestand jedoch in der *Frage der Bundesstaatlichkeit*: Schon vor Kriegsende hatte es hier deutliche Differenzen zwischen den Alliierten und auch innerhalb der einzelnen Regierungen gegeben, wobei der Wunsch nach einer konsequenten Dezentralisierung jedoch durchgehend Pate stand: Während der Sowjetunion auf den Kriegskonferenzen noch die Aufteilung Deutschlands in mehrere Einzelstaaten vorschwebte, was den Vorstellungen des amerikanischen Finanzministers Morgenthau ebenso entgegenkam wie zeitweiligen ähnlichen britischen Konzepten, plädierte das Außenministerium der USA eher für einen Bundesstaat.

Nach 1945 erfuhren diese Pläne durch die gewandelten weltpolitischen Rahmenbedingungen allerdings gravierende Änderungen: Stalin setzte sich nunmehr für die Schaffung eines deutschen Einheitsstaates ein, den er langfristig in das sowjetische Imperium zu integrieren gedachte. Die Amerikaner präferierten jetzt einen konföderalen Bundesstaat mit deutlicherer institutioneller und kompetenzmäßiger Trennung zwischen Bundes- und Landesebene, wobei das föderale Verfassungsgefüge der USA selbst als Vorbild diente.

Die Briten machten sich nun für einen unitarischen Bundesstaat nach Weimarer Vorbild stark, was ihrer eigenen zentralistischen Tradition eher entgegenkam und zudem die Möglichkeit bot, dieses einheitlichere Deutschland besser als Widerpart gegen den sowjetischen Imperialismus einsetzen zu können; Frankreich schließlich setzte sich nun zeitweise für eine Staatenbundlösung ein – ein einheitliches Deutschland mutete unmittelbar nach 1945 zu bedrohlich an und ließ Erinnerungen an das erneute Erstarken des östlichen Nachbarn nach 1918 wach werden.

3.4 Die Verfassungspläne der deutschen Parteien

Auch die deutschen Parteien, die sich nach 1945 wieder bzw. neu konstituiert hatten, waren über die Gestalt der neuen Verfassungsordnung keineswegs einig. „Every leading German has a constitution in his pocket", wie ein Berater des US-Militärgouverneurs Lucius D. Clay die Szenerie leicht belustigt charakterisierte. Im Folgenden kann das Meinungsspektrum daher nur summarisch skizziert werden.

Von den extremistischen Parteien am linken und am rechten Spektrum abgesehen waren sich die demokratischen Parteien jedoch einig, wieder ein parlamentarisches Regierungssystem in der Tradition der Weimarer Verfassung zu schaffen, das allerdings dessen Risiken konsequent vermied. Und insoweit verwundert nicht, dass einerseits an etlichen Stellen Anleihen aus der Verfassung von 1919 gemacht wurden, wo sie auch jetzt noch als Vorbild dienen konnte. Das betraf die Verankerung der Grundrechte ebenso wie das Institutionengefüge, das in seiner allgemeinen formalen Struktur (zweikammeriges Parlament, Kanzler und Regierung, Präsident, bundesstaatliche Ordnung) mit in das Grundgesetz übernommen wurde.

Verändert werden sollten jedoch die Kompetenzen dieser Institutionen und ihre Beziehungen zueinander, um damit gefährliche Elemente der Weimarer Reichsverfassung zu vermeiden: Das Notverordnungsrecht des Staatsoberhaupts wurde getilgt, und nunmehr wurde dieses auch nicht mehr direkt vom Volk gewählt; ein konstruktives Misstrauensvotum sollte zur Regierungsstabilität beitragen und häufige Kabinettsstürze in Zukunft verhindern; ein starkes Verfassungsgericht sollte zudem als 'Wächter' die Einhaltung der Verfassungsgrundsätze prüfen.

Der größte Dissens unter den Parteien bestand jedoch, wie bei den Siegermächten auch, hinsichtlich des Föderalismus: Von der Forderung nach einem Einheitsstaat bis hin zum Plädoyer für einen Bund souveräner Einzelstaaten fand sich im Grunde für jedes Ordnungsmodell auch eine eigene Partei, wobei die genannten Extrempole mit der KPD (Einheitsstaat) und der Bayernpartei (Staatenbund) aber nur schwach besetzt waren.

Dazwischen jedoch tat sich eine heterogene Szenerie auf: Die FDP machte sich für einen dezentralen Einheitsstaat stark, während die CSU für einen konföderalen Bundesstaat eintrat. Auch die CDU forderte einen Bundesstaat, jedoch mehr unitarischen Charakters, womit sie entsprechenden Vorstellungen der SPD nahe kam. Bei dieser Charakterisierung ist allerdings zu berücksichtigen, dass die einzelnen Parteien selbst keineswegs einheitlich gefügt waren; vielfältige Meinungsverschiedenheiten zwischen Parteiflügeln kamen hinzu und verkomplizierten die Szenerie weiter.

Schließlich gab es auch Dissens über die Zusammensetzung der Länderkammer: Hier plädierte die SPD zunächst für eine Komposition nach dem Senatsmodell, wobei sie sich von der Unabhängigkeit der gewählten Landesabgeordneten ein geringeres Vetopotential der Landesregierungen gegen bundespolitische Projekte erhoffte; dies entsprach auch ihrem unitarischen Bundesstaatsmodell, in welchem die Kontrolle der Bundesregierung durch die Länder erkennbar eingeschränkt bleiben sollte. Die CSU und Teile der CDU votierten dagegen für die Bundesratslösung, um den bundespolitischen Einfluss der Landesregierungen möglichst effektiv zu gestalten.

Die heute im Grundgesetz festgeschriebene „abgeschwächte Bundesratslösung" ist Folge eines Kompromisses: Zwar gab die SPD schließlich im Kern nach; jedoch ist der Bundesrat nicht als vollwertige zweite Kammer konstruiert, indem er nur bei *zustimmungspflichtigen* Gesetzen über ein absolutes Vetorecht verfügt. Alle übrigen Gesetze können durch Überstimmen eines Bundesratsvetos in Form eines bekräftigenden Beschlusses durch den Bundestag doch noch in Kraft treten.

3.5 Die Entstehung des Grundgesetzes

Den offiziellen 'Startschuss' zur Erarbeitung einer neuen Verfassung, die durch die inzwischen vollzogene Teilung Deutschlands allerdings nur im Westen des Landes Gültigkeit erlangen würde, gaben schließlich am 1. Juli 1948 die Militärgouverneure Frankreichs, Großbritanniens und der USA mit der Übergabe der Frankfurter Dokumente an die Ministerpräsidenten der westdeutschen Bundesländer.

Darin fand sich der Auftrag, einen Konvent einzuberufen, welcher eine neue deutsche Verfassung ausarbeiten sollte. Die inhaltlichen Vorgaben der Alliierten waren bewusst allgemein gehalten; verbindlich vorgeschrieben wurde nur die Schaffung eines demokratischen und föderalistischen Rechtsstaates, in welchem die individuellen Grundrechte verfassungsrechtlich abzusichern waren.

Dieser Auftrag stieß bei den Ministerpräsidenten nicht auf ungeteilte Zustimmung. Sie hegten die Befürchtung, mit der Erarbeitung und Verabschiedung einer westdeutschen Verfassung die deutsche Teilung zu besiegeln. Es gelang ihnen in der Folge, dem Verfassungsgebungsprozess durch eine Vermeidung des Terminus „Verfassung" den Charakter des Vorläufigen, Provisorischen zu verleihen: Einberufen wurde zum einen lediglich ein „Parlamentarischer Rat", der zudem nicht aus direkt gewählten Mitgliedern bestand, sondern sich aus Abgeordneten der einzelnen Landtage zusammensetzte. Zudem erhielt das erarbeitete Dokument am Ende den neutraleren Namen „Grundgesetz", um auch damit die Vorläufigkeit des Verfassungsgebungsprozesses zu verdeutlichen.

Freilich war sich die Mehrheit der Verfassungsgeber einig, dass die materiellen Bestimmungen auch in einer künftig zu verabschiedenden gesamtdeutschen Verfassung Bestand haben sollten; insoweit war man sich schon frühzeitig im Klaren, dass mit diesem 'Provisorium' inhaltlich schon weitgehend die endgültige Ordnung des neuen Deutschlands festgeschrieben worden war, welche es zu gegebener Zeit auch auf den Osten des Landes auszudehnen galt. Lediglich eine Minderheit, angeführt vom SPD-Vertreter Carlo Schmid, plädierte für die Option einer künftigen Fundamentalrevision dieses „Grundgesetzes" und hielt daher auch inhaltlich an der Fiktion des Verfassungsprovisoriums fest.

Der Entwurf des Grundgesetzes wurde von einem Expertengremium erarbeitet, welches von den Ministerpräsidenten gebildet worden war. Dieser „Herrenchiemseer Konvent", benannt nach dem Tagungsort, stellte die Vorlage im August 1948 fertig. Von September 1948 bis Mai 1949 diskutierte dann der Parlamentarische Rat die Vorlage, wobei insbesondere die schon skizzierten parteipolitischen Meinungsverschiedenheiten die komplizierten Verhandlungen prägten.

Der letztlich gefundene Kompromiss fand eine sehr breite Mehrheit: Bis auf die KPD unterzeichneten alle dort vertretenen Parteien das Dokument; selbst CSU und Bayernpartei, die das festgeschriebene Föderalismusmodell immer noch ablehnten und maßgeblich zur Ablehnung des Grundgesetzentwurfs durch den Bayerischen Landtag beigetragen hatten, stimmten nun zu.

Da somit die Zustimmung des Parlamentarischen Rates vorlag und später auch die Mehrheit der westdeutschen Landtage den Entwurf billigte (nur Bayern hatte dagegen votiert), konnte das Grundgesetz am 23. Mai 1949 in Kraft treten. Eine abschließende Volksabstimmung war nicht vorgesehen, um einmal mehr den provisorischen Charakter des erarbeiteten Dokuments zu unterstreichen. Der spätere große Erfolg des Grundgesetzes ließ derlei Vorbehalte jedoch schon bald in der Versenkung verschwinden.

4. Struktur, Prinzipien und Staatsziele

Das Grundgesetz kann also als Resultat verschiedener Entwicklungen verstanden werden: Erstens spiegelt sich in ihm die deutsche Verfassungstradition, indem zentrale Elemente früherer deutscher Verfassungen (Föderalismus, parlamentarisches Regierungssystem, Bundesratsmodell etc.) erneut aufgegriffen wurden.

Zweitens ist es von verbindlichen inhaltlichen Vorgaben der westlichen Siegermächte geprägt, die den Verfassungsgebern explizit die Schaffung eines föderalistischen Rechtsstaates auftrugen. Und drittens ist es als Kompromissdokument zu verstehen, in welchem die oft recht divergierenden politischen Vorstellungen der einzelnen deutschen Parteien zu einem Ausgleich gebracht wurden.

Im Folgenden sollen nun Aufbau, Prinzipien und Staatsziele des Grundgesetzes genauer unter die Lupe genommen werden, wobei der Verankerung des politischen Institutionengefüges und der Definition und Zuweisung der Staatsaufgaben an diese einzelnen Institutionen besondere Aufmerksamkeit zuteil werden soll.

4.1 Der Aufbau des Grundgesetzes

Nebst einer Präambel, welche die „Verantwortung" des deutschen Volkes „vor Gott und den Menschen" beschwört und seinen Willen bekräftigt, „als gleichberechtigtes Mitglied in einem vereinten Europa dem Frieden der Welt zu dienen", ist das Grundgesetz in 14 Abschnitte gegliedert, die alle bis auf den ersten der Schaffung der Institutionen und Regelung ihrer Beziehungen dienen. In Übersicht 1 sind sie zusammengestellt.

Übersicht 1: Die Gliederung des Grundgesetzes

I.	Die Grundrechte
II.	Der Bund und die Länder
III.	Der Bundestag
IV.	Der Bundesrat
IVa.	Gemeinsamer Ausschuss
V.	Der Bundespräsident
VI.	Die Bundesregierung
VII.	Die Gesetzgebung des Bundes
VIII.	Die Ausführung der Bundesgesetze und die Bundesverwaltung
VIII a.	Gemeinschaftsaufgaben, Verwaltungszusammenarbeit
IX.	Die Rechtsprechung
X.	Das Finanzwesen
X a.	Verteidigungsfall
XI.	Übergangs- und Schlussbestimmungen

Alliiertem Auftrag und eigenem Selbstverständnis gemäß wurde der Grundrechtskatalog, der sich in der vorangegangenen Weimarer Verfassung erst im zweiten Hauptteil fand, bewusst an den Anfang gerückt, um die dem Menschen dienende Funktion von Recht und Staat besonders zu betonen. Die ersten 19 Artikel des Grundgesetzes definieren diese Rechte im Detail, machen aber auch verbindliche Vorgaben zu Möglichkeiten ihrer Einschränkung, wenn es die Wahrung der staatlichen Ordnung erfordert.

Der zweite große Teil des Grundgesetzes, der die Abschnitte II bis VI umfasst, etabliert die bundesstaatliche Ordnung (II) und schafft die für das Regierungssystem entscheidenden Verfassungsorgane Bundestag, Bundesrat, Bundespräsident und Bundesregierung (III, IV, V, VI). Darüber hinaus findet sich hier ein erst im Jahre 1968 eingefügter Abschnitt IV a, welcher einen „Gemeinsamen Ausschuss" aus Bundestag und Bundesrat etabliert, der im Verteidigungsfall als 'Notparlament' und als Garant von Legalität auch in Krisenzeiten fungieren soll.

Der dritte Block, welcher die Abschnitte VII bis VIII a beinhaltet, regelt sodann detailliert die Zusammenarbeit zwischen den Verfassungsorganen im Felde der Gesetzgebung, wobei der Kompetenzabgrenzung zwischen Bund und Ländern gesonderte Beachtung zukommt. Darüber hinaus finden sich Festlegungen zur Ausführung der Bundesgesetze und zur Organisation der Bundesverwaltung. Ein 1969 eingefügter Abschnitt VIII a definiert zusätzlich „Gemeinschaftsaufgaben" (regionale Wirtschaftsförderung, Verbesserung der Agrarstruktur und des Küstenschutzes) von Bund und Ländern, die insbesondere der stärkeren Inpflichtnahme des Gesamtstaates für die regionale Aufgabenerfüllung dienen.

Zuletzt finden sich noch Abschnitte (IX – XI), die den übrigen Teilen nicht unmittelbar zugeordnet werden können. Hier ressortieren Bestimmungen zur Organisation der Rechtsprechung und insbesondere des Bundesverfassungsgerichts (IX), das das 'Fünfeck' der Verfassungsorgane komplettiert, und zur Organisation des Finanzwesens. Ein erst 1968 eingefügter Abschnitt X a dient der Notfallregelung für den Verteidigungsfall, gefolgt von einem umfangreichen Katalog von Übergangsbestimmungen.

Dort finden sich u.a. Vorschriften zur Länderneugliederung, zur Fortgeltung alten Rechts und zur Geltungsdauer des Grundgesetzes, welches außer Kraft tritt, wenn „eine Verfassung in Kraft tritt, die von dem deutschen Volk in freier Entscheidung beschlossen worden ist" (Art. 146). Zudem wurden die Artikel 136 bis 139 sowie 141 der Weimarer Reichsverfassung, die der Regelung des Verhältnisses von Kirche und Staat dienen, durch Artikel 140 wortgleich in das Grundgesetz übernommen.

4.2 Die Prinzipien des Grundgesetzes

Dieser verfassungsrechtlichen Basis liegen wiederum *allgemeine demokratietheoretische Prinzipien* zugrunde, die auch die konkrete Ausformung des bundesdeutschen Institutionengefüges maßgeblich beeinflusst haben. Aus der Erfahrung des Scheiterns der

Weimarer Republik und des Abgleitens in ein totalitäres Unrechtsregime zogen die Verfassungsgeber nicht nur die Konsequenz, das Grundgesetz als positives Gegenteil des totalen Staates zu konzipieren, sondern diese Demokratie auch wehrhaft zu machen.

Und deshalb ist durch Artikel 20 Abs. (4) – im Unterschied zur Weimarer Verfassung von 1919 – jedem Bundesbürger das grundsätzliche Recht auf Widerstand gegen jede Kraft verliehen, welche sich die Beseitigung dieser grundgesetzlichen Ordnung zum Ziel gesetzt hat. Auch den einzelnen politischen Institutionen wurden, wie später noch genauer darzulegen sein wird, weitreichende Rechte zur Verteidigung dieser Ordnung an die Hand gegeben: verfassungsfeindliche Parteien und sonstige Organisationen können nach präzise vorgegebenen Verfahren verboten werden.

Aber nicht nur in bloßer Abgrenzung vom Totalitarismus sind die Leitprinzipien des Grundgesetzes entstanden. Sie speisen sich vielmehr aus einer schon wesentlich älteren, eigenständigen Tradition, wie das Bundesverfassungsgericht im KPD-Verbotsurteil 1956 richtig formulierte: „Das Grundgesetz bezeichnet die von ihm geschaffene Staatsordnung als eine freiheitliche Demokratie. Es knüpft damit an die Tradition des 'liberalen bürgerlichen Rechtsstaats' an, wie er sich im 19. Jahrhundert allmählich herausgebildet hat und wie er in Deutschland schließlich in der Weimarer Verfassung verwirklicht worden ist" (BVerfGE 5: 197).

Der Wesenskern dieser „*Freiheitlichen demokratischen Grundordnung*" (FdGO) ist daher allgemeiner Natur und nicht nur im Grundgesetz verwirklicht, sondern in allen pluralistischen Demokratien. Die FdGO ist dabei als eine Ordnung zu definieren, „die unter Ausschluss jeglicher Gewalt- und Willkürherrschaft eine rechtsstaatliche Herrschaftsordnung auf der Grundlage der Selbstbestimmung des Volkes nach dem Willen der jeweiligen Mehrheit und der Freiheit und der Gleichheit darstellt" (BVerfGE 2: 1), wie das Bundesverfassungsgericht ebenfalls in einem Parteiverbotsurteil – nun gegen die rechtsextremistische Sozialistische Reichspartei (SRP) – im Jahre 1952 formulierte. Im Einzelnen fallen nach dieser klassisch gewordenen Definition folgende Einzelprinzipien unter die FdGO:

- die Achtung der Menschenrechte;
- die Volkssouveränität;
- die Gewaltenteilung;
- die Verantwortlichkeit der Regierung;
- die Gesetzmäßigkeit der Verwaltung;
- die Unabhängigkeit der Gerichte;
- das Mehrparteienprinzip;
- Chancengleichheit aller Parteien „mit dem Recht auf verfassungsmäßige Bildung und Ausübung einer Opposition".

Aus diesem allgemeinen Prinzipienkatalog lassen sich zwar keine präzisen Vorgaben zu den einzelnen Institutionen ableiten; jedoch wurde bei der

Erarbeitung des Grundgesetzes besonders darauf geachtet, Struktur und Zweckbestimmung aller Institutionen FdGO-gemäß zu fassen und ihre Prinzipien besonders zu berücksichtigen.

Insoweit verwundert es nicht, dass neben dem umfangreichen Grundrechtskatalog gerade die Passagen zur Kompetenzabgrenzung zwischen den einzelnen Organen (Gewaltenteilung), zu den Beziehungen zwischen Bundestag und Bundesregierung (Verantwortlichkeit der Regierung), zum Gesetzesvollzug (Gesetzmäßigkeit der Verwaltung) und zur Rechtsprechung (Unabhängigkeit der Gerichte) besonders umfangreich und detailliert ausgefallen sind: Dies sind die Kernprobleme politischer Ordnungen, deren konkrete Regelung im Grundgesetz durch die allgemeinen Maßgaben der FdGO entscheidend beeinflusst sind.

Darüber hinaus nimmt das Grundgesetz insoweit eine Präzisierung vor, indem es der deutschen Demokratie einen *bundesstaatlichen* und einen *sozialstaatlichen* Charakter verleiht (Art. 20 Abs. (1)) und diese Kriterien auch für unabänderlich erklärt (Art. 79 Abs. (3)). Für eine freiheitliche demokratische Grundordnung ist im Prinzip weder das eine noch das andere naturnotwendig: Demokratien können eben auch bewusst als *Einheitsstaaten* konzipiert sein (z.B. Frankreich vor der Regionalisierung) oder sich explizit nicht als Anstalt individueller Daseinsvorsorge verstehen (USA vor dem New Deal), ohne dabei den FdGO-Wesenskern zu verletzen.

Die Tatsache aber, dass es in Deutschland doch erfolgte, hatte sowohl für die Institutionenarchitek-

tur generell (Bund-Länder-Beziehungen) als auch
für die Aufgabenkataloge der einzelnen Institutionen (Pflicht zu wohlfahrts- und sozialpolitischen
Maßnahmen) entscheidende Konsequenzen.

4.3 Die Staatsziele des Grundgesetzes

Schließlich sind im Grundgesetz noch etliche *konkrete Staatsziele* verankert, die das Kompetenzprofil
und die Aufgabenfelder der einzelnen Institutionen
ebenfalls vorprägen. Nicht alle von ihnen fanden
schon 1949 Eingang; manche wurden erst später
durch entsprechende Grundgesetzänderungen eingefügt, als durch geänderte politische Rahmenbedingungen bzw. Wandlungen der politischen Kultur hierfür die Voraussetzungen geschaffen waren.
Im Einzelnen finden sich folgende Staatsziele:

- Wiedervereinigung (Präambel); seit 1949, 1990
  nach der Verwirklichung getilgt;
- Friedenspflicht (Art. 1, 9, 24, 26); erste Bestimmungen 1949, seither mehrmals ergänzt;
- Europäische Integration; Zusammenarbeit in
  und mit internationalen Organisationen (Art. 23,
  24, 28, 45, 50, 53, 76, 88, 115); erste Bestimmungen 1949, seither mehrmals ergänzt;
- Gewährleistung gesamtwirtschaftlichen Gleich-
  gewichts (Art. 109-115); 1967/69 eingefügt;

- Geschlechtliche Gleichberechtigung (Art. 3); seit 1949, 1994 präzisiert (Durchsetzungs*pflicht* des Staates);
- Gleichberechtigung von Behinderten (Art. 3); 1994 eingefügt;
- Umweltschutz (Art. 20 a); 1994 eingefügt;
- Tierschutz (Art. 20a); 2002 eingefügt.

Insgesamt bedeutet dies, dass die Funktionen staatlicher Daseinsvorsorge und Sicherung wirtschaftlichen und gesellschaftlichen Wohlstands seit 1949 gegenüber den klassischen Ordnungsfunktionen (Aufrechterhaltung der öffentlichen Ordnung, Verteidigung, Rechtspflege) noch einmal deutlich angewachsen sind.

Dies hatte unmittelbare Auswirkungen auf die einzelnen politischen Institutionen, denn das angewachsene Aufgabenfeld zog die Schaffung neuer Gremien bzw. Ämter nach sich, welche deren Bewältigung dienen sollten (u.a. Umweltministerien auf Bundes- und auf Landesebene, Gleichberechtigungs- und Behindertenbeauftragte in allen öffentlichen Ämtern, Bildung eigener Europaausschüsse in den Parlamenten bzw. entsprechender Ministerien).

5. Stellung und Aufgaben der Institutionen

Diese allgemeinen Prinzipien und Ziele des Grundgesetzes hatten also maßgeblichen Einfluss auf die konkrete Ausformung der Institutionenordnung, da sie die einzelnen Verfassungsorgane vorbestimmten, die Regelung ihrer Beziehungen bedingten sowie eine Präzisierung ihrer Aufgaben erforderlich machten. Im Folgenden sollen verfassungsrechtliche Stellung, Aufgaben und Funktionen der einzelnen Institutionen herausgearbeitet werden, wobei die fünf Verfassungsorgane Bundestag, Bundesregierung, Bundesrat, Bundespräsident und Bundesverfassungsgericht im Fokus stehen.

5.1 Das Institutionengefüge im Überblick

Eine große Zahl von Institutionen des Bundes besitzt Verfassungsrang (vgl. Übersicht 2). Dabei war den Vätern und Müttern des Grundgesetzes nicht an einer vollständigen Aufzählung aller für die Organisation des Staates notwendigen Einrichtungen gelegen; vielmehr waren sie davon geleitet, nur die wichtigsten verfassungsrechtlich zu legitimieren. Es verwundert daher nicht, dass die Liste dieser 'privilegierten' Institutionen etwas willkürlich wirkt; allerdings war der Gesetzgeber bestrebt, die grundgesetzliche Verankerung durch die Formulierung des jeweiligen Artikels besonders zu begründen.

Übersicht 2: Die Institutionen im Grundgesetz

Institutionen	GG-Artikel
I. Bund, Länder, Kommunen	
Bundesstaatliche Ordnung im allgemeinen	20 (1)
Volksvertret. in Ländern, Kreisen, Gemeinden	28 (1)
II. Bundestag	
Bundestag	38, 39
Ausschuss für Angelegenheiten der EU	45
Ausschuss für auswärtige Angelegenheiten	45a
Ausschuss für Verteidigung	45a
Wehrbeauftragter	45b
Petitionsausschuss	45c
Parlamentarisches Kontrollgremium	45d
III. Bundesrat	
Bundesrat	50, 51
Europakammer des Bundesrates (optional)	52 (3a)
IV. Zusammenarbeit von Bundestag und Bundesrat	
Vermittlungsausschuss	77
Gemeinsamer Ausschuss	53a
V. Bundespräsident und Bundesregierung	
Bundespräsident	54
Bundesregierung	62
Bundeskanzler	63
Bundesminister der Verteidigung	65a
VI. Bundeseigene Verwaltung, Streitkräfte	
Auswärtiger Dienst, Bundesfinanzverwaltung, Bundeswasserstraßen- und Schifffahrtsverwaltung	87 (1)

Bundesgrenzschutz, Zentralstellen für polizeiliche Auskunft und Nachrichtenwesen, Kriminalpolizei, Verfassungsschutz (optional)	87 (1)
Bundesunmittelbare Träger der Sozialversicherung	87 (2)
Bundeswehr	87a
Bundeswehrverwaltung	87b
Bundeseigene Luftverkehrsverwaltung	87d
Bundeseigene Eisenbahnverkehrsverwaltung	87e
Bundeseigene Verwaltung im Bereich der Wahrnehmung hoheitlicher Aufgaben des Postwesen und der Telekommunikation	87 f
Bundeswasserstraßenverwaltung	89
Finanzverwaltung	108 (1)
Bundesautobahn- und -straßenverwaltung	90
VII. Rechtsprechung des Bundes	
Bundesverfassungsgericht	92, 94
Oberste Bundesgerichte (Bundesgerichtshof, Bundesverwaltungsgericht, Bundesfinanzhof, Bundesarbeitsgericht, Bundessozialgericht)	95
Gemeinsamer Senat der Obersten Bundesgerichte	95 (3)
Finanzgerichtsbarkeit	108 (6)
Bundesgericht für gewerblichen Rechtsschutz, Wehrstrafgerichte, Disziplinargerichte (optional)	96
VIII. Bundesbank und Bundesrechnungshof	
Bundesbank	88
Bundesrechnungshof	114
Quelle: Eigene Zusammenstellung; gelistet sind nur die zur Schaffung der Institution wesentlichen Artikel	

Dabei ist zu betonen, dass viele der heute geltenden Bestimmungen erst nach 1949 durch entsprechende Änderungen bzw. Ergänzungen Eingang in das Grundgesetz fanden. Insoweit präsentiert der vorliegende Abschnitt eine aktuelle Momentaufnahme. Da spätere Passagen der genaueren Erläuterung der einzelnen Einrichtungen dienen, sei an dieser Stelle nur das Gesamtmuster des grundgesetzlichen Institutionengefüges beleuchtet.

Ganz erkennbar stehen die fünf Verfassungsorgane Bundestag, Bundesrat, Bundesregierung, Bundespräsident und Bundesverfassungsgericht im Fokus. Vier von ihnen sind eigene Unterabschnitte gewidmet; das Bundesverfassungsgericht wird nur im Rahmen des allgemeinen Abschnitts IX „Rechtsprechung" verankert, nimmt dort aber einen prominenten Platz ein.

Darüber hinaus waren die Verfassungsgeber bestrebt, die Kooperation zwischen dem Bundestag und dem Bundesrat, die bei der Gesetzgebung zu enger Zusammenarbeit genötigt sind, durch Vermittlungsinstanzen zu institutionalisieren, sowohl für den politischen Normalfall (Vermittlungsausschuss) als auch für Notstandszeiten (Gemeinsamer Ausschuss). Auch in vielen anderen Artikeln sind die Beziehungen zwischen den Verfassungsorganen detailliert geregelt.

Weiterhin finden sich umfangreiche Bestimmungen zum Aufbau einer bundeseigenen Verwaltung, die aus dem bundesstaatlichen Verbundmodell des Grundgesetzes herrühren: Grundsätzlich verbrieft die Verfassung den Bundesländern die Ausführung von Bundesgesetzen „als eigene Angelegenheit" (Art. 83), wofür sie ihre eigenen Verwaltungen einsetzen.

„Soweit dieses Grundgesetz nichts anderes bestimmt oder zulässt", lautet jedoch der zweite Teil des Artikels, und er bedingt, dass alle in Bundeszuständigkeit fallenden Verwaltungsaufgaben deshalb auch einzeln benannt werden müssen. Ein langer Katalog, vom Auswärtigen Dienst über die Bundesfinanzverwaltung bis hin zur Bundeswehr und zur Bundeswasserstraßenverwaltung ist so zusammengekommen, welcher das Spektrum oberer Bundesbehörden festlegt.

Die Generalklausel des Artikels 87 Abs. (3) impliziert zudem, dass je nach Erfordernis „für Angelegenheiten, für die dem Bunde die Gesetzgebung zusteht, selbständige Bundesoberbehörden und neue bundesunmittelbare Körperschaften und Anstalten des öffentlichen Rechtes durch Bundesgesetz errichtet werden" können. Das schafft genügend Flexibilität für die Gestaltung der bundesunmittelbaren Verwaltung, ohne den Grundsatz der Länderzuständigkeit zu verletzen.

Auch die Rechtsprechung findet detaillierte Regelung, wobei nicht nur das Bundesverfassungsgericht dort seine Verankerung findet, sondern auch die Obersten Bundesgerichte (Bundesgerichtshof, Bundesverwaltungsgericht, Bundesfinanzhof, Bundesarbeitsgericht und Bundessozialgericht). Weiterhin werden durch Artikel 92 auch die Gerichte der Länder explizit in dieses System eingebunden sowie durch Artikel 108 Abs. (6) die einheitliche bundesgesetzliche Regelung der Finanzgerichtsbarkeit vorgeschrieben.

Bundesbank und Bundesrechnungshof wurden durch eigene Artikel ebenfalls grundgesetzlich verankert, was ihre Sonderstellung und ihre Weisungsunabhängigkeit betonen soll. Zwar finden sich detaillierte Bestimmungen hierzu in den entsprechenden Artikeln 88 und 114 selbst nicht, sind aber in Bundesgesetzen verankert, deren Schaffung für den Bundesrechnungshof vom Grundgesetz sogar verbindlich vorgeschrieben ist.

Seit 1992 findet sich hier jedoch im Gefolge der Errichtung der Wirtschafts- und Währungsunion der Europäischen Union ein Passus, der die Übertragung von Aufgaben und Befugnisse der Bundesbank an die Europäische Zentralbank (EZB) ermöglicht, was mit der Einrichtung der EZB zum 1. Juni 1998 auch erfolgte.

5.2 Der Bundestag

Es ist kein Zufall, dass der Bundestag in der Reihenfolge der Verfassungsorgane als erster seine verfassungsrechtliche Verankerung findet. Damit soll der herausgehobenen Stellung der Volksvertretung auch symbolisch Rechnung getragen werden — keine Selbstverständlichkeit, wenn man dagegen die Verfassung der Fünften Französischen Republik von 1958 betrachtet, in welcher das Parlament erst nach dem Staatspräsidenten und der Regierung behandelt wird, was die dominierende Position der

46

Exekutive im System des dortigen „rationalisierten Parlamentarismus" spiegelt.

Abschnitt III des Grundgesetzes, der die Artikel zum Deutschen Bundestag umfasst, dient zunächst der Absicherung der Rechte seiner Mitglieder, was sowohl der verfassungsgeschichtlichen Tradition als auch der totalitären Erfahrung des Dritten Reiches Rechnung trägt: Der vielzitierte und -diskutierte Artikel 38 definiert die Abgeordneten zunächst als „Vertreter des ganzen Volkes", die „an Aufträge und Weisungen nicht gebunden und nur ihrem Gewissen unterworfen" sind.

Parlamentarismuskritik will aus diesem Artikel bis heute herauslesen, dass jegliche Form von Fraktionsdisziplin diesem Grundsatz widerspräche und die grundgesetzlich normierte Entscheidungsfreiheit des einzelnen Parlamentariers einenge. In der Praxis zeigt sich jedoch, dass nur in Ausnahmefällen (Abtreibungsrecht, Beteiligung an Friedensmissionen etc.) die Abgeordneten einen entsprechenden Gewissenskonflikt haben, der sie in Gegensatz zur herrschenden Meinung ihrer eigenen Fraktion bringt. Nicht von ungefähr wird in solchen Fällen bei Abstimmungen häufig die Fraktionsbindung aufgehoben, um die Konfliktlage zu entschärfen.

Darüber hinaus trägt das Grundgesetz dem individuellen Schutz der Abgeordneten gezielt Rechnung. Zum einen verankert Artikel 46 die Grundsätze der Indemnität (Straffreiheit) und der Immunität (Freiheit von Strafverfolgungsaktivitäten) der Parlamentarier: „Ein Abgeordneter darf zu keiner Zeit wegen seiner Abstimmung oder wegen einer

Äußerung, die er im Bundestage oder in einem seiner Ausschüsse getan hat, gerichtlich oder dienstlich verfolgt oder sonst außerhalb des Bundestages zur Verantwortung gezogen werden", bestimmt Artikel 46 Abs. (1), nimmt davon jedoch ausdrücklich „verleumderische Beleidigungen" aus, um den politischen Diskurs von persönlichen Fehden und Wortwechseln freizuhalten.

Abs. (2) ermöglicht es dem Bundestag außerdem, die Immunität einzelner Abgeordneter aufzuheben, um sie für die Strafverfolgung zugänglich zu machen. Damit wird deutlich, dass das Grundgesetz den Parlamentariern keinen unbegrenzten Freibrief erteilt hat, sondern ein verantwortungsvoller Umgang mit den zugeteilten Rechten erwartet wird.

Gleiches gilt sinngemäß für ihr Zeugnisverweigerungsrecht gemäß Artikel 47, das sich nur auf Personen bezieht, „die ihnen in ihrer Eigenschaft als Abgeordnete oder denen sie in dieser Eigenschaft Tatsachen anvertraut haben sowie über diese Tatsachen selbst". Es gilt also nur für Sachverhalte im Zusammenhang mit ihrer Abgeordnetentätigkeit und kann deshalb nicht zur generellen Zeugnisverweigerung auch in Privatsachen instrumentalisiert werden.

Die übrigen Artikel machen Vorgaben zur Wahl und zur Organisation des Bundestages, sind aber bewusst allgemein gehalten, um Ausgestaltungsfreiheit sowohl für Ausführungsgesetze (z.B. Bundeswahlgesetz) als auch für die Geschäftsordnung des Bundestages zu lassen – auch dies keine Selbstverständlichkeit, wenn man erneut die französische

Verfassung zum Vergleich heranzieht, wo sich detaillierte Normen zur Parlamentsorganisation und zur Gesetzgebung finden, die zur Machtbeschränkung der Abgeordneten dienen.

Und so schreibt das Grundgesetz im Wesentlichen nur die Dauer der Wahlperiode, die allgemeinen Grundsätze des Wahlrechts sowie das Recht zur Wahlprüfung fest: Gemäß Artikel 39 Abs. (1) wird der Bundestag auf vier Jahre gewählt; die Wahlperiode endet erst mit dem Zusammentritt eines neuen Bundestages, was ein 'parlamentsloses' Interregnum verhindert. Nur in Ausnahmefällen ist eine vorzeitige Auflösung des Bundestages möglich (vgl. Art. 68 GG).

Die Parlamentarier sind gemäß Artikel 38 Abs. (1) „in allgemeiner, unmittelbarer, freier, gleicher und geheimer Wahl" zu bestimmen; wahlberechtigt (aktives Wahlalter) ist man gemäß Abs. (2) mit vollendetem 18. Lebensjahr, wählbar (passives Wahlrecht) mit dem Eintritt der „Volljährigkeit", also gegenwärtig mit demselben Alter.

Alle übrigen Bestimmungen, insbesondere zum Wahlsystem, sind im Bundeswahlgesetz bzw. in der Bundeswahlordnung niedergelegt und genießen daher keine verfassungsrechtliche Absicherung. Über die Gültigkeit der Wahl entscheidet der Bundestag gemäß Artikel 41 schließlich selbst und kann dabei auch den Verlust der Mitgliedschaft eines Abgeordneten formell feststellen. Allerdings ist dies vor dem Bundesverfassungsgericht anfechtbar.

Vergleichbar allgemein sind auch die Organisationsgrundsätze gehalten, die das Grundgesetz dem

Bundestag auferlegt: Artikel 40 schreibt die Wahl eines Präsidiums sowie den Erlass einer Geschäftsordnung vor und skizziert kurz die Aufgaben des Bundestagspräsidenten (Hausrecht und Polizeigewalt im Bundestagsgebäude). Artikel 42 verankert die grundsätzliche Öffentlichkeit parlamentarischer Beratungen; nur mit Zweidrittelmehrheit kann auf Antrag von zehn Prozent der Bundestagsmitglieder oder der Bundesregierung die Öffentlichkeit ausgeschlossen werden, was jedoch bei Plenardebatten noch nie zur Anwendung gekommen ist.

Allerdings schreibt § 69 der Geschäftsordnung des Bundestags (GOBT) demgegenüber grundsätzlich die Nichtöffentlichkeit von Ausschussberatungen fest; die Zulassung des Publikums zu den Beratungen muss im Einzelfall mit einfacher Mehrheit beschlossen werden – ein durchaus umstrittenes Prozedere. Nach herrschender Lehre und geltendem Recht bezieht sich der Öffentlichkeitsgrundsatz des Grundgesetzes also nur auf die Plenardebatten.

Der Aufbau der Parlamentsorganisation liegt im Übrigen weitgehend im Ermessen des Bundestages. Jedoch genießen bestimmte Gremien bzw. Ämter Verfassungsrang und müssen daher obligatorisch eingerichtet werden. Das gilt für einen „Ausschuss für die Angelegenheiten der Europäischen Union" (Art. 45) und den „Ausschuss für Auswärtige Angelegenheiten" (Art. 45a) ebenso wie für den Verteidigungsausschuss (Art. 45a), den Wehrbeauftragten (Art. 45b), den Petitionsausschuss (Art. 45c) und das Parlamentarische Kontrollgremium zur Beaufsichtigung der nachrichtendienstlichen Tätigkeit des Bundes (Art. 45d).

Darüber hinaus ist das Recht des Bundestags zur Einsetzung von Untersuchungsausschüssen festgeschrieben, die auf Antrag schon eines Viertels der Bundestagsmitglieder zu konstituieren sind und damit ein wichtiges Kontrollinstrument der jeweiligen Opposition darstellen.

5.3 Die Bundesregierung

Auch die grundgesetzlichen Vorgaben zur Organisation der Bundesregierung sind recht allgemein gehalten. Gemäß Artikel 62 besteht sie als Kollegialorgan aus dem Bundeskanzler und den Bundesministern. „Das Amt des Bundeskanzlers oder eines Bundesministers endigt in jedem Falle mit dem Zusammentritt eines neuen Bundestages, das Amt eines Bundesministers auch mit jeder anderen Erledigung des Amtes des Bundeskanzlers", schreibt Artikel 69 weiter vor. Während ihrer Amtszeit dürfen die Regierungsmitglieder „kein anderes besoldetes Amt, kein Gewerbe und keinen Beruf ausüben" (Art. 66) und zudem nicht zur Leitung eines Unternehmens gehören. Aufsichtsratsmandate bedürfen der Zustimmung des Bundestages.

Artikel 62 folgend gehören weder die beamteten noch die im Jahre 1969 geschaffenen parlamentarischen Staatssekretäre der Bundesregierung formell an; letztere sind jedoch *faktisch* längst ein Teil von ihr, da sie die Ressortchefs häufig in Kabinettssitzungen vertreten.

Einzelheiten über die Rechtsstellung der Bundesminister und der parlamentarischen Staatssekretäre sowie über die Arbeitsorganisation von Kabinett und Ministerialverwaltung sind darüber hinaus sowohl in einzelnen Gesetzen (Bundesministergesetz, Gesetz über die Parlamentarischen Staatssekretäre) sowie in der Geschäftsordnung der Bundesregierung und in der Gemeinsamen Geschäftsordnung der Bundesministerien festgelegt.

Rechnung trugen die Verfassungsgeber jedoch der grundgesetzlichen Verankerung der drei Organisationsgrundsätze der Bundesregierung, die sich mit den Begriffen Kanzlerprinzip, Kabinettsprinzip und Ressortprinzip fassen lassen: Ersteres verbrieft dem Bundeskanzler eine Richtlinienkompetenz innerhalb des Kabinetts; Artikel 65 gemäß bestimmt der Regierungschef „die Richtlinien der Politik und trägt dafür die Verantwortung".

Sie findet jedoch ihre Grenzen im Ressortprinzip, dem gemäß „innerhalb dieser Richtlinien ... jeder Bundesminister seinen Geschäftsbereich selbständig und unter eigener Verantwortung" leitet, was zumindest verfassungsrechtlich das willkürliche 'Hineinregieren' des Kanzlers in die Ressorts seiner Minister begrenzt. Freilich ist dies sehr von den jeweiligen Personen abhängig, und gerade führungsstarke Regierungschefs, wie etwa Konrad Adenauer, Helmut Schmidt oder Helmut Kohl, haben sich in der Praxis oft wenig darum geschert.

Sinngemäß gilt dies auch für das Kabinettsprinzip: Gemäß Artikel 65 entscheidet bei Meinungsverschiedenheiten zwischen Ministern die Bundesregierung als Ganzes, nicht der Kanzler. Und auch sonstige Beschlüsse, insbesondere über Gesetzesvorlagen, werden vom Kabinettskollegium insgesamt gefasst, was die Dominanz des Kanzlers in der politischen Praxis jedoch ebenfalls nicht ausschließt.

Denn unter Kanzler Helmut Schmidt etwa mutierten Kabinettssitzungen regelmäßig zu Examensveranstaltungen, in welchen die einzelnen Bundesminister zum Rapport anzutreten und ihre Vorlagen vom Regierungschef prüfen zu lassen hatten, was allerdings die Entwicklung eines „sachbezogenen Teamgeistes" (Klaus von Beyme) in der Ministerrunde nicht verhinderte.

Die übrigen Bestimmungen zur Bundesregierung betreffen im Wesentlichen die Wahl und Abwahl des Kanzlers durch den Bundestag, die später noch genauer betrachtet werden sollen. Hinzuweisen ist schließlich noch auf die besondere verfassungsrechtliche Verankerung des Bundesministers der Verteidigung (Art. 65a) und die Festschreibung seiner Befehls- und Kommandogewalt über die Streitkräfte, die jedoch nur im Frieden gilt und im Verteidigungsfall auf den Bundeskanzler übergeht.

5.4 Der Bundesrat

Die grundgesetzliche Verankerung des Bundesrates fällt noch wesentlich kürzer aus und reflektiert das Bestreben der Verfassungsgeber, dem Geist des Föderalismus auch durch ein weitreichendes Recht der Länder zur Selbstorganisation ihrer Kammer Rechnung zu tragen. Lediglich vier Grundgesetzartikel machen daher nur sehr allgemeine Vorgaben.

Grundsätzliche Verbriefung findet zunächst das Recht zur Mitwirkung „bei der Gesetzgebung und Verwaltung des Bundes und in Angelegenheiten der Europäischen Union" (Art. 50), wobei der EU-Passus erst 1992 Eingang in die Verfassung fand. Immerhin konstituieren diese dürren Bestimmungen das Recht des Bundesrats auf die obligatorische Mitwirkung an der Bundesgesetzgebung, was allerdings in der Folge noch durch etliche weitere Artikel (70-82) genauer gefasst wird.

Darüber hinaus ist die Zusammensetzung der Länderkammer gemäß Artikel 51 nach dem Bundesratsprinzip festgeschrieben: „Der Bundesrat besteht aus Mitgliedern der Regierungen der Länder, die sie bestellen und abberufen. Sie können durch andere Mitglieder ihrer Regierungen vertreten werden."

Damit unterliegen die einzelnen Ländervertreter einem imperativen Mandat und der permanenten Pflicht zur Rechenschaft. Seit der Wiedervereinigung stehen jedem Bundesland je nach Einwohnerzahl drei bis sechs Stimmen zu, wobei diese nur einheitlich abgegeben werden können; vor 1990 galt ein anderer Verteilungsschlüssel mit Kontingenten zwischen drei und fünf Stimmen.

Der Bundesrat hat zudem gemäß Artikel 52 einen Präsidenten zu wählen, der jeweils ein Jahr amtiert. Er hat die Kammer einzuberufen, „wenn die Vertreter von mindestens zwei Ländern oder die Bundesregierung es verlangen". In der Praxis rotiert das Amt nach einem festgelegten Schlüssel unter den einzelnen Regierungschefs der Länder. Schließlich besitzt auch die bereits 1988 durch die Geschäftsordnung des Bundesrates zur Beratung von EG-Vorlagen eingerichtete „Europakammer" seit 1992 Verfassungsrang, „deren Beschlüsse als Beschlüsse des Bundesrates gelten". In der politischen Praxis spielt dieses Gremium jedoch nur eine untergeordnete Rolle, da sich das Bundesratsplenum bisher die Masse der Beschlussvorlagen selbst vorbehalten hat.

Alles Übrige, insbesondere die Organisation des Ausschusssystems, wird in der Geschäftsordnung des Bundesrates geregelt, wobei Artikel 52 Abs. (4) noch die Möglichkeit eröffnet, „andere Mitglieder oder Beauftragte der Regierungen der Länder" in die Ausschüsse zu entsenden. Sie sind daher in der Regel mit Länderbeamten besetzt, welche die Beschlussvorlagen für das Plenum erarbeiten und damit zum eigentlichen Arbeitsort der Länderkammer geworden sind.

5.5 Der Bundespräsident

Die Bestimmungen des Grundgesetzes zum Bundespräsidenten machen nur wenige Vorgaben zur Organisation und zur personellen Qualifikation für dieses Verfassungsorgan. Wesentlich genauer sind demgegenüber das Wahlverfahren sowie die Kompetenzabgrenzung zu anderen Verfassungsorganen geregelt.

Gemäß Artikel 54 Abs. (1) ist jeder Deutsche für dieses Amt wählbar, „der das Wahlrecht zum Bundestage besitzt und das vierzigste Lebensjahr vollendet hat". Diese hohe Altershürde sollte sicherstellen, dass nur reife Persönlichkeiten mit hohem politischem Ansehen Berücksichtigung finden. Bis heute ist diese Rechnung meistens aufgegangen, hat aber auch dazu geführt, das Bundespräsidentenamt als 'Austragsstelle' für angehende 'Politrentner' zu missbrauchen: Bei etlichen bisherigen Amtsinhabern (u.a. Heinrich Lübke, Gustav Heinemann, Karl Carstens, Roman Herzog, Johannes Rau) und auch dem derzeit amtierenden Frank-Walter Steinmeier war von vornherein klar, dass ihre Wahl zwar einerseits die protokollarische Krönung ihrer politischen Karriere bildete, andererseits aber auch deren Ende.

Die Parteien sind daher immer wieder versucht, alternde Spitzenfunktionäre in dieses Amt 'wegzuloben', um damit der Folgegeneration den Einstieg in Regierungsämter zu erleichtern. Dieses traditionelle Muster ist allerdings im letzten Jahrzehnt mit dem noch recht jungen Christian Wulff bzw. den politischen Seiteneinsteigern Horst Köhler und Joachim Gauck merklich aufgeweicht worden.

Die Amtszeit beträgt fünf Jahre, wobei nur eine Wiederwahl zulässig ist. In bewusster Absetzung von der Weimarer Reichsverfassung wird der Bundespräsident nicht vom Volk direkt, sondern durch die Bundesversammlung gekürt, welche sich gemäß Artikel 54 Abs. (3) aus den Bundestagsabgeordneten „und einer gleichen Anzahl von Mitgliedern, die von den Volksvertretungen der Länder nach den Grundsätzen der Verhältniswahl gewählt werden", zusammensetzt. Dieser eigenwillige Wahlmodus sollte nach den Vorstellungen der Verfassungsgeber das politische Gewicht des Staatsoberhauptes begrenzen, welches gerade in der Weimarer Republik durch seine direkte plebiszitäre Legitimation aktive Eingriffe in das Regierungshandeln rechtfertigen konnte.

Möglichem Amtsmissbrauch ist darüber hinaus durch Artikel 61 vorgebeugt, der die Anklage des Bundespräsidenten vor dem Bundesverfassungsgericht „wegen vorsätzlicher Verletzung des Grundgesetzes oder eines anderen Bundesgesetzes" ermöglicht. Berechtigt dazu sind jedoch nur Bundestag oder Bundesrat, welche eine Anklage mit Zweidrittelmehrheit beschließen müssen, was einen lagerübergreifenden Konsens erfordert.

Das Bundesverfassungsgericht könnte anschließend das Staatsoberhaupt seines Amtes entheben, wenn es dazu die erforderlichen Tatbestände feststellt. Bis heute musste dieses Regularium erfreulicherweise nicht zur Anwendung kommen, da demokratische Gesinnung sowie verfassungskonforme Amtsführung bei allen Amtsinhabern außer Frage standen.

Für seine Amtsgeschäfte steht dem Staatsoberhaupt mit dem Bundespräsidialamt eine eigene behördliche Organisation zur Verfügung, die jedoch keine grundgesetzliche Verankerung besitzt, sondern durch ein einfaches Gesetz geschaffen wurde. Es unterstützt ihn bei der Wahrnehmung seiner Funktionen, zu denen die völkerrechtliche Vertretungskompetenz (Art. 59), die Ernennung von Beamten, Soldaten und Richtern des Bundes (Art. 59) und die Ausübung seines Gnadenrechts (Art. 60) ebenso gehören wie die weiter unten genauer zu erörternde Mitwirkung im Gesetzgebungsprozess.

Auch die formelle Ernennung und Entlassung des Bundeskanzlers und der Bundesminister sowie die Auflösung des Bundestages sind präsidiale Befugnisse, in der regulären politischen Praxis jedoch meist „staatsnotarieller" Natur (Wolfgang Rudzio). In politischen Krisenzeiten ermöglicht ihm die Rechtsordnung jedoch einen erheblichen Kompetenzzuwachs – sogenannte „Reservefunktionen".

5.6 Das Bundesverfassungsgericht

Auch die grundgesetzlichen Vorgaben zur Organisation des Bundesverfassungsgerichts sind auffallend kurz gehalten. Neben dem generellen Auftrag zu dessen Einrichtung (Art. 92) sind in Artikel 94 nur sehr allgemeine Grundsätze festgeschrieben: Es

58

hat sich aus „Bundesrichtern und anderen Mitgliedern" zusammenzusetzen, wobei die Verfassungsrichter je zur Hälfte vom Bundestag und vom Bundesrat zu wählen sind, um politische Gleichberechtigung von Bund und Ländern im Besetzungsverfahren sicherzustellen.

Konkrete persönliche Qualifikationsvoraussetzungen für diese Ämter sind im Grundgesetz selbst nicht festgeschrieben; dagegen legt es besonderes Augenmerk darauf, die richterliche Unabhängigkeit (Art. 97) zu betonen: Die 'Hüter des Gesetzes' unterliegen keinen Weisungen, sondern sind „nur dem Gesetze unterworfen".

Alle organisatorischen Details sind jedoch erst durch das Bundesverfassungsgerichtsgesetz festgelegt worden: Hier wurde die Amtszeit der Richter auf zwölf Jahre ohne Wiederwahlmöglichkeit festgeschrieben, um die parteipolitische Unabhängigkeit der Mitglieder sicherzustellen. Trotz der Wahl der Richter durch parteipolitisch geprägte Organe ist diese Rechnung in der Tat weitgehend aufgegangen: Ein systematisch parteipolitisch gefärbtes Rechtsprechungsverhalten der Richter konnte bislang nicht nachgewiesen werden, auch wenn in der Vergangenheit bestimmte Verfassungsgerichtssenate immer wieder als „rot" oder „schwarz" gefärbt tituliert wurden.

Darüber hinaus war es Sache von Bundestag und Bundesrat, durch die Geschäftsordnungen ihre eigenen Wahlverfahren festzulegen: Während der Bundesrat schon seit jeher als Plenum darüber befindet, besaß der Bundestag dazu über etliche Jahrzehnte einen parteipolitisch proportional besetzten Richterwahlausschuss. Seit 2015 wird aber auch dort im Plenum über die Richterkandidaten abgestimmt. In beiden Organen ist jedoch eine Zweidrittelmehrheit für die Wahl nötig, was eine Verständigung über die politischen Lager hinweg erforderlich macht und im Regelfall zur Nominierung kompromissfähiger Kandidaten und zu einer konsensuellen Wahl führt.

Möglich wurde dies durch Befolgung eines Besetzungsproporzes, bei welchem den beiden Großparteien ein informelles Nominierungsrecht für einen Teil der Richter eingeräumt wird, die durchweg auch *Parteimitglieder* sind; den Kleinparteien gelang es dagegen nur selten, eigene Kandidaten durchzusetzen. Im Regelfall folgen die anderen Parteien diesen Nominierungen; Ausnahmen gab es jedoch, wie etwa die 1993 abgeblockte Wahl der SPD-Politikerin Herta Däubler-Gmelin, deren Wille zur parteipolitischen Unabhängigkeit von der Union in Zweifel gezogen wurde.

Auch die Gliederung in zwei Senate mit jeweils acht Richtern, die Abgrenzung ihrer Zuständigkeiten sowie der Aufbau eines administrativen Unterbaus ist erst im Bundesverfassungsgerichtsgesetz geregelt: So ist der Erste Senat als „Grundrechtssenat" für Entscheidungen über Verfassungsbeschwerden und Normenkontrollanträge mit Bezug zum Grundrechtskatalog (Art. 1-17 GG) zuständig, der Zweite Senat als „Staatsrechtssenat" für Entscheidungen über Organ- und Bund-Länder-Streitverfahren, sonstige Normenkontrollen und Verfassungsbeschwerden, Parteiverbote und die Wahlprüfung.

Einzelheiten des Verfahrensablaufs sind darüber hinaus in der Geschäftsordnung des Gerichts festgelegt. Genauere Festlegungen trifft das Grundgesetz demgegenüber nur bei den verfassungsgerichtlichen Zuständigkeiten, die wegen ihres engen Bezugs zur Tätigkeit anderer Verfassungsorgane aber erst weiter unten betrachtet werden sollen.

6. Konkurrenz und Kooperation der Organe

Die Schaffung einzelner Institutionen durch das Grundgesetz zieht die Notwendigkeit nach sich, ihre Beziehungen zueinander zu klären. Die entsprechenden Bestimmungen haben die Grundsätze der Kooperation festzulegen und auch den Modus des Konfliktaustrags zu definieren. Im Folgenden sollen die verfassungsrechtlichen Vorgaben dazu genauer untersucht werden, wobei das Beziehungsgeflecht zwischen den fünf Verfassungsorganen im Mittelpunkt steht.

6.1 Bundestag und Bundesregierung

Die Kooperation und auch die personelle Verflechtung zwischen Bundestag und Bundesregierung, die in einem parlamentarischen Regierungssystem unabdingbar sind, werden durch die Bestimmungen des Grundgesetzes gezielt gefördert. Zwar müssen Bundeskanzler und Bundesminister nicht ausdrücklich Bundestagsmitglieder sein, sind dies jedoch in der Regel, da das Parlament gemäß Artikel 63 Abs. (1) den Regierungschef auf Vorschlag des Bundespräsidenten wählt und damit seine 'Personalhoheit' sicherstellt.

Bis auf Kurt Georg Kiesinger besaßen daher alle Bundeskanzler ein Parlamentsmandat, und auch die überwiegende Mehrheit der Bundesminister. Sollte der Vorschlag des Staatsoberhaupts keine Mehrheit finden – bei klaren Mehrheitsverhältnissen im Parlament höchst unwahrscheinlich und daher bis heute noch nicht eingetreten – kann auch jemand anderes zum Kanzler gewählt werden.

Den schlechten Weimarer Erfahrungen folgend ist die Abwahl des Kanzlers in der laufenden Legislaturperiode gemäß Artikel 67 nur durch ein konstruktives Misstrauensvotum, also durch die Wahl eines Nachfolgers möglich, was Kontinuität in der Regierungsarbeit sicherstellen soll. Durch die hohen Hürden, die ein derartiges Verfahren für die Amtsenthebung setzt, ist ein 'Kanzlersturz' heute sehr unwahrscheinlich geworden.

Möglich ist er allerdings, wenn eine Regierungskoalition zerfällt bzw. ihre parlamentarische Mehrheit zu verlieren droht: ersteres war Voraussetzung des einzigen erfolgreichen konstruktiven Misstrauensvotums, als die FDP im Jahr 1982 aus der sozialliberalen Koalition ausschied und im neuen Bündnis mit der Union Helmut Kohl formell zum Nachfolger Helmut Schmidts wählte. Dagegen scheiterte 1972 der Versuch von CDU und CSU, die geschwächte SPD/FDP-Koalition unter Willy Brandt durch die Wahl ihres Fraktionsvorsitzenden Rainer Barzel zu stürzen. Bis heute sind dies die einzigen Fälle solcher konstruktiven Misstrauensanträge geblieben.

Parlamentarische Kontrollrechte gegenüber der Bundesregierung sind darüber hinaus noch in Artikel 43 verankert: Kabinettsmitglieder können gemäß Abs. (1) vom Plenum bzw. von Ausschüssen jederzeit herbeizitiert werden, um gewünschte Auskünfte zu geben. Auch diese Festschreibung ist im

Regelfall von geringer praktischer Bedeutung, da Kanzler und Minister ohnehin in sehr engem Kontakt mit dem Parlament stehen, insbesondere natürlich mit ihren eigenen Fraktionen.

Bedeutsam wird dieses Recht allenfalls, wenn es um die Vorladung von Regierungsmitgliedern vor Untersuchungsausschüsse geht; aber auch dann ist ein Herbeizitieren nur möglich, wenn es die Mehrheit des Ausschusses beschließt. Und da die Untersuchungsausschüsse nach dem Parteienproporz des Plenums zusammengesetzt sind, verfügt die Regierungsmehrheit auch dort über eine Majorität und kann von der Opposition gewünschte Vorladungen abschmettern.

Spiegelbildlich dazu existieren auch verschiedene Einwirkungsmöglichkeiten der Bundesregierung auf das Parlament. Gleichfalls in Artikel 43 ist zunächst das Zutritts- und Anhörungsrecht der Regierungsmitglieder festgeschrieben – ein Passus, der gerade für Kabinettsangehörige ohne Bundestagsmandat von Bedeutung ist, die ansonsten zumindest formell keinen Zutritt zum Bundestag hätten. Darüber hinaus ist dieses Recht gemäß Abs. (2) auch „Beauftragten" der Regierung verliehen, was die verfassungsrechtliche Basis für die heute übliche permanente Präsenz von Ministerialbeamten in Ausschusssitzungen darstellt.

Die Gesetzgebungsarbeit des Parlaments kann die Regierung verfassungsrechtlich darüber hinaus durch ihr Gesetzesinitiativrecht beeinflussen, das in Art 76 Abs. (1) verankert ist. Auch diese formelle Garantie ist praktisch unnötig, da heute ohnehin die Masse der Gesetzesprojekte vonseiten der Regierung und ihrer Ministerialbürokratie kommt, ja deren Vorlage von den Parlamentariern sogar erwartet wird. Mit anderen Worten: Selbst ohne formelle Verankerung eines Gesetzesinitiativrechts der Regierung würden diese Vorlagen den Weg in das Parlament finden, dann eben aber informell, wie dies in den USA bei präsidentiellen Entwürfen gängige Praxis ist.

Unter bestimmten, bewusst eng begrenzten Bedingungen kann der Kanzler schließlich die Auflösung des Bundestages herbeiführen, um Neuwahlen zu ermöglichen. Artikel 68 Abs. (1) ermöglicht dies, wenn eine Vertrauensfrage des Kanzlers nicht von der Mehrheit der Parlamentsmitglieder (Kanzlermehrheit) positiv beschieden wird. Gedacht ist es für Fälle fehlender parlamentarischer Mehrheiten, welchen durch Neuwahlen abgeholfen werden soll. In diesem Falle kann der Kanzler den Bundespräsidenten um die Auflösung des Bundestages bitten, wobei das Staatsoberhaupt hierzu aber nicht verpflichtet ist, sondern einen gewissen Ermessensspielraum besitzt.

Fragwürdige Anwendung fand dieses Verfahren zum einen nach der 'Wende' 1982, als der neu gewählte Kanzler Helmut Kohl es zur Durchsetzung vorzeitiger Neuwahlen instrumentalisierte: Nach Stellung der Vertrauensfrage wurde für die Regierungsfraktionen von CDU/CSU und FDP Stimmenthaltung vereinbart, was ein Negativvotum vorprogrammierte, da die sozialdemokratische Opposition erwartungsgemäß gegen Kohl stimmte.

Bundespräsident Carstens (CDU) entsprach sodann dem Wunsch des Bundeskanzlers nach Parlamentsauflösung, obwohl Kohl faktisch noch über eine stabile Bundestagsmehrheit verfügte. Nicht zu Unrecht warf man Carstens daher später eine parteiliche Nutzung seines Ermessensspielraums vor. Eine Klage in Karlsruhe gegen die Auflösung scheiterte allerdings.

Bundeskanzler Schröder nutzte das Verfahren nach der für die SPD im Frühjahr 2005 verlorenen Landtagswahl in Bundesland Nordrhein-Westfalen ebenfalls, um bundespolitisch für klare parteipolitische Verhältnisse zu sorgen: Ohne die Mehrheit im Bundestag verloren zu haben, fingierte auch er bei der Vertrauensabstimmung durch Stimmenthaltung seiner Koalition eine Abstimmungsniederlage, um vorzeitige Wahlen herbeizuführen. Folge war diesmal allerdings die Niederlage der rot-grünen Bundesregierung. Insoweit ist dieses Verfahren jenseits seiner politischen Instrumentalisierbarkeit durchaus riskant.

6.2 Bundestag und Bundesrat

Bundestag und Bundesrat sind nach dem Willen der Verfassungsgeber vor allem auf dem Felde der Gesetzgebung zur Zusammenarbeit genötigt, was in der politischen Praxis zu einem faszinierenden Machtpoker zwischen beiden Verfassungsorganen geführt hat. Ein eigener Abschnitt des Grundgesetzes mit nicht weniger als dreizehn zum Teil sehr detaillierten Artikeln dient der Regelung des Gesetzgebungsprozesses und der Kompetenzabgrenzung zwischen Bund und Ländern.

Jedoch ist die Aufteilung der Zuständigkeiten zwischen beiden Ebenen bewusst nicht trennscharf erfolgt, sondern mit einer breiten Palette an Gesetzgebungsfeldern, die der *konkurrierenden Gesetzgebung* unterliegen: Hier „haben die Länder die Befugnis zur Gesetzgebung, solange und soweit der Bund von seiner Gesetzgebungszuständigkeit nicht durch Gesetz Gebrauch gemacht hat", wie Artikel 72 Abs. (1) das zugrunde liegende Prinzip definiert. Artikel 74 listet sodann inzwischen nicht weniger als 33 Gebiete auf, die vom Personenstandswesen und der Regelung von Ausbildungsbeihilfen über die Krankenhausförderung bis hin zum Arbeitsrecht reichen.

Die auf diesen Feldern erlassenen Normen machen heute die Masse aller Bundesgesetze aus, zumal der Bund über die Jahrzehnte hinweg von dieser Generalvollmacht systematisch Gebrauch gemacht und die Länderzuständigkeiten systematisch zurückgedrängt hat. Allerdings hat man diesem Trend durch die Föderalismusreform I des Jahres 2006 und dabei insbesondere durch die Abschaffung der bundeseinheitlichen Rahmengesetzgebung (ersatzlose Streichung von Art. 75 GG) entgegengewirkt.

Demgegenüber fallen die Kataloge ausschließlicher Gesetzgebungszuständigkeiten von Bund bzw. Ländern kürzer aus. Artikel 73 listet vierzehn exklusiv in Bundeszuständigkeit fallende Bereiche auf, von denen die Regelung der auswärtigen Angelegenheiten, des Währungswesens und des Luftverkehrs zu den wichtigsten gehören. Ausschließliche Landeszuständigkeiten, wie das Kultur- und Bildungswesen und die Polizei, sind dagegen nicht ausdrücklich aufgelistet, sondern ergeben sich konkludent aus verschiedenen anderen Artikeln (insbesondere 91a und b).

Durch die 1969 eingefügten „Gemeinschaftsaufgaben" von Bund und Ländern gemäß Artikel 91a (Hochschulbau, inzwischen getilgt; regionale Wirtschaftsförderung; Verbesserung der Agrarstruktur und Küstenschutz) sind die Spielräume der Bundesländer aber auch in diesen Zuständigkeitsbereichen einengbar.

Im Kontext dieses komplexen Kompetenzszenarios hat nun der Bundesrat als Länderkammer an der Bundesgesetzgebung mitzuwirken und gleichzeitig einer unkontrollierten Vereinnahmung von Landeszuständigkeiten durch den Bund vorzubeugen. Grundsätzlich ist ihm das leicht möglich, da er an jedem Gesetzgebungsverfahren auf Bundesebene obligatorisch zu beteiligen ist. Allerdings ist nur bei *zustimmungspflichtigen Gesetzen* (insbes. Grundgesetzänderungen und das Bund-Länder-Verhältnis betreffende Normen) ein positives Votum der 'Länderkammer' absolut erforderlich; in den übrigen Fällen kann der Bundestag das Veto des Bundesrates gemäß Artikel 77 Abs. (4) mit einfacher bzw. mit Zweidrittelmehrheit zurückweisen.

Da die Zahl der zustimmungspflichtigen Gesetze über die Jahrzehnte jedoch deutlich angestiegen ist und sich bis zur Jahrtausendwende im Schnitt auf weit über 50 Prozent belief, ist der bundespolitische Einfluss der Länderkammer ebenso angewachsen. Erst die Föderalismusreform I von 2006 hat hier zu einer Brechung dieses Unitarisierungstrends geführt.

Gemäß Artikel 80 Abs. (2) haben diese Entwicklungen im Übrigen auch Konsequenzen für den Erlass von Rechtsverordnungen des Bundes, da solche, die der Ausführung zustimmungspflichtiger Gesetze dienen, ebenfalls der Billigung durch den Bundesrat bedürfen.

Die Architekten der Verfassung haben vorausgesehen, dass aus dieser Konstellation ernsthafte Konflikte zwischen den Kammern entstehen könnten. Und deshalb sahen sie in Artikel 77 Abs. (2) die Möglichkeit der Bildung eines Vermittlungsausschusses vor, der mit Bundestags- und Bundesratsvertretern zu besetzen und dessen Zusammensetzung und Verfahren durch die Geschäftsordnung des Bundestages mit Zustimmung des Bundesrates zu regeln ist. Diese segensreiche Einrichtung hat dazu geführt, dass seit 1949 nur ein Bruchteil der Gesetzesvorlagen an der Uneinigkeit beider Kammern gescheitert ist.

6.3 Bundesregierung und Bundesrat

Bundesregierung und Bundesrat geraten durch das Grundgesetz nicht direkt in Konkurrenz und Kooperationszwang, wohl aber mittelbar. Denn zum einen zeichnet faktisch die Regierung für die große Masse bundesgesetzlicher Vorlagen verantwortlich, für welche sie auch die Zustimmung des Bundesrates benötigt bzw. welche zumindest von der Länderkammer obligatorisch zu beschließen sind.

Hinzu kommt, dass der Bundesrat gemäß Artikel 76 Abs. (1) selbst Gesetzentwürfe einbringen kann, welche Bundestag und insbesondere die Bundesregierung politisch unter Zugzwang setzen können. Dasselbe gilt nach Artikel 80 Abs. (3) für die Vorlage von Verordnungsentwürfen zu verabschiedeten zustimmungspflichtigen Gesetzen. Zwar hält sich im Regelfall das prozentuale Aufkommen an Bundesratsinitiativen deutlich in Grenzen: zwischen 1949 und 1994 etwa belief sich der Anteil von Gesetzentwürfen der Länderkammer durchschnittlich auf gerade einmal 6,6 Prozent.

Jedoch erfährt dieses Instrument gerade in Zeiten oppositioneller Bundesratsmehrheiten eine signifikante Aufwertung: In diesem Szenario entwickelt sich ein enger Kooperationsverbund aus der parlamentarischen Minderheit des Bundestages und den 'befreundeten' Landesregierungen im anderen Haus.

Dies führt regelmäßig zu einem Anwachsen oppositioneller Gesetzesvorlagen aus der Länderkammer und zu einer Vergrößerung ihrer Realisierungschancen, da die Bundestagsminderheit nunmehr in der guten Lage ist, mit der Blockade durch die eigene Bundesratsmehrheit drohen zu können. Um eigene Projekte, zustimmungspflichtige zumal, nicht unnötig zu gefährden, ist daher die jeweilige

Bundesregierung in einer solchen Konstellation zu einer deutlich kooperativeren Gangart gegenüber dem Bundesrat genötigt.

Regelmäßig versucht sie dabei aber auch, einzelne Länder aus einer ablehnenden Front herauszubrechen, was ihr gerade im Falle koalitionsregierter Bundesländer mit Regierungsbeteiligung einer Partei des eigenen Lagers immer wieder gelingt. Insbesondere große Koalitionen aus CDU und SPD, wo naturgemäß immer ein Partner auch der Führungspartei der Bundesregierung zugehört, sind hierfür besonders anfällig.

Gelingt es dem Kanzler in einem solchen Falle, die eigene Landespartei 'auf Linie' und gegen den dortigen Regierungspartner in Stellung zu bringen, sehen die Koalitionsverträge regelmäßig die Stimmenthaltung im Bundesrat vor, was das Bröckeln der gesamten Oppositionsfront fördert.

Offene Verletzungen solcher Verträge, wie durch den brandenburgischen Ministerpräsidenten Stolpe bei der Abstimmung über das Zuwanderungsgesetz am 22. März 2002, sind dabei nur seltene Ausnahmen von der Regel, zumal sie ernsthafte Koalitionskrisen im betroffenen Bundesland zur Folge haben, an denen beiden Regierungspartnern letztlich nur wenig gelegen sein kann.

6.4 Bundesregierung, Bundestag und Bundespräsident

Bundesregierung, Bundestag und Bundespräsident sind durch das Grundgesetz sowohl auf dem Felde der Gesetzgebung als auch im Bereich der Regierungsbildung und der Wahrnehmung exekutiver Befugnisse zur Zusammenarbeit verpflichtet, wobei die politische Federführung der jeweiligen Bundesregierung und ihrer parlamentarischen Mehrheit zukommt.

An der Gesetzgebung ist der Bundespräsident im Regelfall nur in 'staatsnotarieller' Funktion beteiligt: Gemäß Artikel 82 Abs. (1) werden die „nach den Vorschriften des Grundgesetzes zustande gekommenen Gesetze (...) vom Bundespräsidenten nach Gegenzeichnung ausgefertigt und im Bundesgesetzblatte verkündet". Formal korrekt zustande gekommene Vorlagen sind daher vom Staatsoberhaupt zu ratifizieren; ein generelles präsidiales Vetorecht hat unser Grundgesetz damit ausdrücklich nicht vorgesehen.

Die Formulierung lässt allerdings die Interpretation zu, dass der Bundespräsident auch im Falle der Verletzung *inhaltlicher Verfassungsnormen* die Ausfertigung eines Gesetzes verweigern kann. Juristisch ist dies bis heute strittig, und doch haben Bundespräsidenten ein derartiges materielles Prüfungsrecht immer wieder beansprucht. So hat etwa Richard von Weizsäcker im Jahre 1991 dem Gesetz zur Privatisierung der Flugsicherung seine Zustimmung verweigert, und auch die 6. Novelle zum Parteiengesetz 1994 fand seine Missbilligung, obwohl er sie schließlich doch ausfertigte und eine nachfolgende Prüfung durch das Bundesverfassungsgericht anmahnte. In diesem engen Rahmen nehmen Bundespräsidenten also durchaus materielle Prüfungen vor.

Der Vollständigkeit halber sei noch darauf verwiesen, dass im Falle einer verlorenen Vertrauensabstimmung und damit fehlender Parlamentsmehrheit des Kanzlers (vgl. Art. 68 zur Rolle des Bundespräsidenten bei einer vorzeitigen Bundestagsauflösung) er gemäß Artikel 81 Abs. (1) „auf Antrag der Bundesregierung mit Zustimmung des Bundesrates für eine Gesetzesvorlage den Gesetzgebungsnotstand erklären [kann], wenn der Bundestag sie ablehnt, obwohl die Bundesregierung sie als dringlich bezeichnet hat". Diese legislativen Notstandsbefugnisse mussten jedoch bis heute nicht bemüht werden.

Bei der Bildung der Regierung ist der Bundespräsident im Regelfall ebenfalls nur in notarieller Funktion tätig. Der durch die vorangegangene Bundestagswahl faktisch zum künftigen Bundeskanzler bestimmte Führer der Parlamentsmehrheit wird dem Bundestag vom Bundespräsidenten gemäß Artikel 63 Abs. (1) dann nur mehr formell zur Wahl vorgeschlagen, wobei die Abgeordneten nicht exklusiv an diesen Vorschlag gebunden sind, sondern in späteren Wahlgängen auch andere Kandidaten aufstellen können.

Nur in Zeiten unklarer parlamentarischer Mehrheiten nach einer Wahl, in denen der künftige Bundeskanzler noch nicht feststeht und durch Sondierungen erst gefunden werden müsste, könnte aus diesem zeremoniellen Recht auch ein politisch gewichtiges werden, da das Staatsoberhaupt sich dann faktisch an der Kandidatenfindung beteiligen könnte – aber nicht müsste.

Bislang ist dieses Szenario aber noch nicht eingetreten, zumal die realistischen Koalitionsoptionen ohnehin begrenzt sind. Verhandlungen dazu führen die Parteien zudem in Eigenregie; eine Einbindung des Bundespräsidenten ist hierbei nicht üblich. Die Ernennung von Kanzler und Ministern durch das Staatsoberhaupt ist am Ende nur mehr Formsache.

Zu ergänzen ist noch, dass ihm laut Artikel 59 die völkerrechtliche Vertretung Deutschlands obliegt: „Er schließt im Namen des Bundes die Verträge mit auswärtigen Staaten" – dies freilich immer unter dem Vorbehalt der Bundesregierung, welcher die außenpolitische Federführung zukommt. Ein international hoch angesehener Bundespräsident, wie etwa Richard von Weizsäcker in den achtziger und frühen neunziger Jahren, kann aber trotz dieses engen Korsetts gerade durch gelungene Auslandsvisiten erheblichen Einfluss auf die deutsche Außenpolitik erlangen.

6.5 Das Bundesverfassungsgericht und die übrigen Organe

Das Bundesverfassungsgericht steht aufgrund seiner Sonderrolle auch in besonderen Beziehungen

74

zu den übrigen Verfassungsorganen. Konstituiert werden diese in erster Linie durch die verschiedenen Verfahrensarten, die den Verfassungsorganen, aber auch anderen Antragsberechtigten zustehen: Je nach Verfahren besitzen gemäß Artikel 93 Abs. (2) und Artikel 100 Abs. (1) die Bundesregierung, eine Landesregierung, ein Viertel der Bundestagsmitglieder, eine Kommune, Gerichte oder auch einzelne Bürger dieses Recht.

Die übrigen Verfassungsorgane bzw. deren Mitglieder tragen dabei im Regelfall Organ- und Bund-Länder-Streitigkeiten aus oder lassen bereits verabschiedete Gesetze durch „abstrakte Normenkontrolle" auf ihre Verfassungskonformität überprüfen. Da es dabei um die Entscheidung von Kompetenzfragen und strittigen Inhalten geht, sind diese Verfahren durchweg hochpolitisch.

So etwa richtete sich der Normenkontrollantrag der Bayerischen Staatsregierung von 1973 gegen den Grundlagenvertrag mit der DDR nicht nur gegen das Vertragsdokument, sondern die Mehrheit der Unionsparlamentarier erhoffte sich von einem Erfolg ihrer Klage auch die Diskreditierung der gesamten Ost- und Deutschlandpolitik der sozialliberalen Koalition: Ihrer Auffassung nach verletzte das Dokument die grundgesetzlich verankerte staatliche Einheit Deutschlands, indem es durch die Anerkennung der DDR-Regierung als völkerrechtliche Vertragspartnerin die Teilung Deutschlands in zwei Staaten besiegelte. Das Gericht folgte letztlich zwar nicht dem Antrag, stellte jedoch klar, dass der Vertrag den Grundsatz des völkerrechtlichen Fortbestandes von Gesamtdeutschland nicht berühre.

Auch Organstreitigkeiten sind durchweg hochpolitisch: So klagten die Bundestagsfraktionen von SPD und Grünen im Jahre 1983 erfolgreich gegen die Bundesregierung, die dem Untersuchungsausschuss zur Aufklärung illegaler Parteienfinanzierung wichtige Dokumente vorenthalten hatte. Die Richter entsprachen dem Antrag und stellten eine Verletzung von Artikel 44 fest, wo insbesondere in Abs. (3) die Verpflichtung von Gerichten und Verwaltungsbehörden zur „Rechts- und Amtshilfe" für Untersuchungsausschüsse des Bundestages festgeschrieben ist.

Da von den illegalen Praktiken in erster Linie die an der Regierung befindliche Union und die FDP profitiert hatten, war dieses Urteil politisch in doppelter Hinsicht schwerwiegend: Zum einen kritisierte es die Vertuschungspraxis der Bundesregierung unter Helmut Kohl, zum anderen erzwang es die Weitergabe belastender Dokumente, die in der Folge das öffentliche Ansehen der Regierung deutlich schädigten.

Hinzuweisen ist zudem noch auf die Möglichkeiten für die Verfassungsorgane bzw. ihre Mitglieder, Grundrechtsverwirkungen für Einzelpersonen und Parteiverbote zu beantragen sowie Präsidenten- und Richteranklagen zu erheben. Relevant sind hiervon bisher lediglich die Parteiverbotsverfahren gemäß Artikel 21 Abs. (2) geworden, durch welche 1952 die neonazistische Sozialistische Reichspartei (SRP) und 1956 die KPD aufgelöst wurden. Nicht

76

von ungefähr nahm das Bundesverfassungsgericht beide Urteile zum Anlass, um in der Begründung Wesenskern und Schutzwürdigkeit der Freiheitlichen demokratischen Grundordnung (FdGO) noch einmal besonders zu betonen.

Wie zweischneidig dieses Schwert politisch ist, zeigen jedoch die beiden NPD-Verbotsverfahren, die letztlich doch nicht zu deren Verbot führen: Denn wenn ein entsprechender Antrag scheitert, kann daraus ein deutlicher Reputationsgewinn extremistischer Parteien erwachsen. Selbst im Falle eines Verbots ist nicht auszuschließen, dass ein Mitleids- bzw. Zorneffekt das Stimmenpotential des rechten parteipolitischen Randes vergrößern würde, allerdings dann anderen Organisationen zugutekäme. Und schließlich können derartige Verbote auch Neugründungen nicht verhindern, wie etwa an der 1968 entstandenen Deutschen Kommunistischen Partei (DKP) als Nachfolgeorganisation der KPD ablesbar.

Durch den großen politischen Einfluss der Verfassungsgerichtsurteile glaubten viele Beobachter schon einen Trend zur „Justizialisierung der Politik" (Christine Landfried) ausmachen zu können, indem bei jeder wichtigen politischen Entscheidung schon ein möglicher 'Gang nach Karlsruhe' antizipiert und die Meinung der Richter quasi in vorauseilendem Gehorsam schon bei der Planung von Vorlagen berücksichtigt werden.

Umfassende Belege für diese These stehen allerdings aus. In jedem Falle aber hat die parteipolitische Aufladung der Entscheidungsverfahren erhebliche Auswirkungen auf die Auswahl der Richter selbst gehabt, die je zur Hälfte vom Bundestag und vom Bundesrat zu bestimmen sind.

7. Änderungen der Institutionenordnung

Die Grundzüge der deutschen Institutionenordnung sind seit Verabschiedung des Grundgesetzes im Jahre 1949 unverändert geblieben, zumal wesentliche Charakteristika (Bundesstaatlichkeit, Gewaltenteilung, Rechtsstaatlichkeit) nicht disponibel sind bzw. der 'Ewigkeitsgarantie' von Artikel 79 Abs. (3) unterliegen. Und doch hat die deutsche Verfassung in den letzten Jahren eine Vielzahl von Änderungen erfahren, die auch substantielle Wandlungen des Institutionengefüges nach sich zogen. Der folgende Abschnitt verschafft einen Überblick über diese Änderungen und stellt die wesentlichen näher vor.

7.1 Die Änderungen im Überblick

Nicht weniger als 60 Änderungen hat das Grundgesetz bis heute erfahren, wie der Übersicht im Anhang im Einzelnen zu entnehmen ist (Stand: April 2017). Nicht alle von ihnen hatten Bedeutung für die Gestalt des bundesdeutschen Institutionensystems, und auch Umfang und Reichweite der vorgenommenen Anpassungen und Ergänzungen differieren ganz erheblich. Die für das Institutionengefüge einschlägigen Änderungen lassen sich folgendermaßen gruppieren:

- Bestimmungen zur *Ergänzung* bzw. zur *Neuordnung* des *Institutionengefüges* durch *Schaffung neuer Einrichtungen* oder durch *Neugliederung des Bundesgebietes.* Hierunter fallen so wichtige Grundgesetzänderungen wie die Wehrverfassung der Jahre 1954 und 1956 zum Aufbau der Bundeswehr und zur Integration der Bundesrepublik in die NATO, die Notstandsgesetzgebung der Großen Koalition von 1968 mit Verfassungszusätzen für den Notstands- und Verteidigungsfall sowie die Grundgesetzreform des Jahres 1994.

  Auch die wiedervereinigungsbedingten Verfassungsänderungen modifizierten das deutsche Institutionengefüge insbesondere durch die Ausweitung des Bundesrates ganz beträchtlich. Und schließlich fallen hierunter mehrere Änderungen zu den territorialen Neugliederungsvorgaben des Grundgesetzes, wie etwa die Sonderbestimmungen für die Länder Berlin und Brandenburg gemäß Artikel 118a.

- Bestimmungen zu *Schaffung, Organisation und Zuständigkeit einzelner Institutionen.* Dazu zählen Festlegungen zur Bundesverwaltung (Zuständigkeiten und Organisation der Bundesfinanzbehörden, Schaffung einer bundesunmittelbaren Luftverkehrsverwaltung, Privatisierung von Bundesbahn und Bundespost), aber auch zur Gerichtsorganisation (Einrichtung von Wehrstrafgerichten, Organisation und Zuständigkeit von Disziplinargerichten, Übertragung von Kompetenzen auf Landesgerichte) und zur Bildung einzelner

Verfassungsorgane (Absenkung des Wahlalters
für Bundestagswahlen auf 18 Jahre, grundgesetzliche Verankerung des Petitionsausschusses des
Bundestages, Bestimmungen zur Bundestags-
wahlperiode). Auch Änderungen bei den Fristen
für die Vorlage bzw. Beratung von Gesetzesvorlagen durch die Bundesregierung und den Bundesrat können hier zugeordnet werden.

- Bestimmungen zur *Kompetenz einzelner Institutionen
  bzw. der Kompetenzabgrenzung.* Hierunter fällt eine
  Fülle von Änderungen bzw. Ergänzungen zur
  bundesstaatlichen Aufgabenwahrnehmung. Bestimmungen zur Reform der Finanzverfassung
  von 1955 und 1970 und die Verteilung des Steu-
  eraufkommens auf Bund, Länder und Kommunen von 1958 finden sich hier ebenso wie Ergänzungen des Katalogs der Konkurrierenden
  Gesetzgebung (z.B. um den Umweltschutz und
  den Tierschutz) und die Einführung der „Gemeinschaftsaufgaben" von Bund und Ländern
  in den Sachgebieten Hochschulbau (inzwischen
  wieder gestrichen), Förderung regionaler Wirt-
  schafts- und Agrarstruktur sowie Küstenschutz.
  Auch die Möglichkeit zur Rückübertragung
  von Gesetzgebungszuständigkeiten auf die Länder, welche im Rahmen der Verfassungsreform
  von 1994 vorgesehen wurde, fällt unter diese
  Rubrik. Diesem Problemkomplex wurde dann
  später durch die Föderalismusrefom I von 2006
  besonders Rechnung getragen, die auch einer
  weiteren Unitarisierung in der Gesetzgebung
  entgegenwirkte. Die Föderalismusreform II von

2009 ergänzte dies durch umfassende Neuregelungen zur Finanzverfassung und zur Verschuldungsbegrenzung von Bund, Ländern und den Kommunen.

Aus alldem wird schon im ersten Überblick ersichtlich, dass das bundesdeutsche Institutionengefüge einem permanenten Wandel unterliegt. Viel davon erfolgt in kleinen Schritten und ist für sich genommen nicht sonderlich gewichtig. Über die Jahrzehnte hinweg summierten sie sich jedoch und ergaben gerade in Kombination mit den wenigen reformerischen Großprojekten einen *Trend zur Unitarisierung* des deutschen Bundesstaates, also zu einer systematischen Ausweitung von Bundeskompetenzen zu Lasten der Länder, der auch durch die Föderalismusreformen des letzten Jahrzehnts nicht effektiv gebrochen wurde.

Im Folgenden sollen nun vier markante Grundgesetzänderungen (Wehrverfassung, Notstandsverfassung, Grundgesetzrefom von 1994, Föderalismusreformen I und II), die die deutsche Institutionenlandschaft markant verändert haben, exemplarisch genauer vorgestellt werden.

7.2 Die Wehrverfassung

Die Einfügung der „Wehrverfassung" in unser Grundgesetz im Jahre 1956 markiert die erste große Verfassungsänderung, welche auch auf das Institutionengefüge deutliche Auswirkungen hatte. Bei der

Verabschiedung der bundesdeutschen Verfassung im Jahre 1949 bestand trotz interner Planungen der ehemaligen Westalliierten und diesbezüglicher Vorbereitungen der Regierung Adenauer selbst keine einheitliche Meinung über die Wünschbarkeit und die Reichweite einer deutschen Wiederbewaffnung sowie zur Integration der Bundesrepublik in die gerade gegründete NATO.

Zwar hatte die erste Bundesregierung schon 1950 mit der Errichtung des „Amtes Blank", das als Keimzelle eines künftigen Verteidigungsministeriums diente, erste Zeichen gesetzt. Jedoch schufen erst die Pariser Verträge von 1955, in denen die deutsche Souveränität bis auf den generellen alliierten Vorbehalt zum Abschluss eines gesamtdeutschen Friedensvertrages festgeschrieben wurde, die rechtliche Basis für den Aufbau eigener Streitkräfte. Gleichzeitig wurde die Aufnahme des Landes in die NATO und in die WEU beschlossen.

Bereits im Jahr zuvor waren im Grundgesetz mehrere Änderungen vorgenommen worden, welche die Grundlage für die eigentliche Wehrverfassung schaffen sollten: In den Katalog der ausschließlichen Gesetzgebungskompetenzen des Bundes (Art. 73 Nr. 1) wurden nun auch die Bereiche „Verteidigung" einschließlich der Wehrpflicht und der Zivilschutz aufgenommen. Nach dem Inkrafttreten der Pariser Verträge und der noch im Jahre 1955 erfolgte Aufnahme der Bundesrepublik in die beiden Verteidigungsbündnisse war der Weg frei für die grundgesetzliche Verankerung der deutschen Wiederbewaffnung. Schon vorher wurde das

Amt Blank in das „Bundesministerium der Verteidigung" umgewandelt (07.06.55), und auch die ersten 101 Freiwilligen der neuen Bundeswehr erhielten schon im November 1955 ihre Ernennungsurkunden, noch bevor die dazu nötige Verfassungsänderung in Kraft getreten war.

Diese erfolgte erst im März 1956 und verankerte die Wehrverfassung durch die Änderung bzw. Neuschaffung von nicht weniger als fünfzehn Artikeln im Grundgesetz. Die zentralen Artikel 87a und b verpflichteten den Bund nunmehr, „Streitkräfte zur Verteidigung" und eine zugehörige Bundeswehrverwaltung aufzustellen. Damit war die Nutzung der Bundeswehr für Angriffskriege von vornherein untersagt. Die allgemeine Wehrpflicht wurde durch die Änderung des Artikels 12 grundgelegt, der die Heranziehung aller deutschen Bürger „im Rahmen einer herkömmlichen allgemeinen, für alle gleichen öffentlichen Dienstleistungspflicht" ermöglichte.

Präzisere verfassungsrechtliche Festlegungen zur Wehrpflicht bzw. für einen entsprechenden Ersatzdienst wurden jedoch erst 1968 durch Anfügung eines neuen Artikels 12a getroffen. Artikel 17a ermöglichte aber schon 1956 eine grundsätzliche gesetzliche Einschränkung des Rechts auf freie Meinungsäußerung, der Versammlungsfreiheit sowie des Petitionsrechts für Wehr- und Ersatzdienstleistende. Entsprechende Begrenzungen waren gemäß Abs. (2) auch für das Freizügigkeitsrecht sowie das Recht auf Unverletzlichkeit der Wohnung zulässig.

Trotz dieser Optionen zur Einschränkung der Grundrechte war den Verfassungsgebern auch an der grundgesetzlichen Garantie menschenwürdiger Führung in den Streitkräften gelegen. Dem neuen Bundeswehr-Konzept der „Inneren Führung" folgend, welches die Formung eines mündigen und demokratisch gesinnten Soldaten bezweckte, wurde zudem noch das Amt des Wehrbeauftragten geschaffen (Art. 45b), der im Auftrag des Deutschen Bundestages als Ombudsmann der Bundeswehrangehörigen fungieren und „zum Schutz der Grundrechte" der Soldaten gegen Vorgesetztenwillkür aktiv werden sollte.

Ein eigener Personalprüfungsausschuss, der allen Beförderungen und Stellenzuweisungen ab dem Dienstgrad Oberst bzw. Kapitän zur See aufwärts zuzustimmen und damit die Formung einer demokratisch gesinnten Generalität sicherzustellen hatte, wurde nun ebenfalls eingerichtet.

7.3 Die Notstandsverfassung

Zwölf Jahre nach Erlass der Wehrverfassung erfolgte die zweite große Grundgesetzreform, die auf das bundesdeutsche Institutionengefüge ebenfalls nachhaltige Auswirkungen hatte. Schon länger bestanden Forderungen nach einer „Notstandsverfassung", welche detaillierte Bestimmungen für Krisenzeiten festschrieb. Im Einzelnen sollten sowohl für den extern induzierten Spannungs- und Verteidigungsfall als auch für den „Inneren Notstand" und den Katastrophenfall präzise verfassungsrechtliche Vorkehrungen getroffen werden.

Erst die überaus breite parlamentarische Bundestagsmehrheit der seit 1966 amtierenden Großen Koalition konnte jedoch die zur Grundgesetzänderung nötigen Zweidrittelmehrheiten in Bundestag und Bundesrat sicherstellen. Die sich zu dieser Zeit voll entfaltende außerparlamentarische Opposition (APO) mit häufig militantem Gepräge bestärkte die beiden Großparteien nur noch in dem Wunsch, auch für den innenpolitischen Krisenfall rechtliche Vorkehrungen zu treffen. Zu diesem Zwecke wurden nicht weniger als 28 Verfassungsartikel geändert bzw. neu in das Grundgesetz aufgenommen. Im Kern schufen sie folgende Neuerungen:

• Artikel 53a verfügte die Schaffung eines „Gemeinsamen Ausschusses" von Bundestag und Bundesrat, der in Krisenzeiten als 'Notparlament' zu fungieren hat, wenn die beiden parlamentarischen Kammern durch die Umstände selbst am Zusammentritt gehindert sind. Gemäß Abs. (1) besteht er zu zwei Dritteln aus Bundestagsabgeordneten und zu einem Drittel aus Bundesratsmitgliedern. „Die Abgeordneten werden vom Bundestage entsprechend dem Stärkeverhältnis der Fraktion bestimmt; sie dürfen nicht der Bundesregierung angehören. Jedes Land wird durch ein von ihm bestelltes Mitglied des Bundesrates vertreten", schreibt derselbe Absatz weiter vor. Im neuen Artikel 115e wurde die Funktion des Gemeinsamen Ausschusses noch weiter präzisiert.

- Auch die Bestimmungen zur Abwehr innerer Bedrohungen wurden nun präzisiert. Der neu gefasste Artikel 91 ermöglichte den Einsatz von Polizeikräften und des Bundesgrenzschutzes „zur Abwehr einer drohenden Gefahr für den Bestand oder die freiheitliche demokratische Grundordnung des Bundes oder eines Landes". Im Bedarfsfall konnten gemäß Artikel 87a Abs. (4) auch die Streitkräfte „beim Schutze von zivilen Objekten und der Bekämpfung organisierter und militärisch bewaffneter Aufständischer" eingesetzt werden, wenn die polizeilichen Kräfte hierzu nicht ausreichten.

- Weiterhin wurden rechtliche Vorkehrungen zur Einschränkung verfassungswidrig wahrgenommener Grundrechte getroffen: Eine Reihe von Änderungen des Grundrechtskatalogs ermöglichten nun u.a. die Einschränkung der Vereinigungsfreiheit, des Post-, Brief- und Fernmeldegeheimnisses sowie der Arbeitsplatzwahlfreiheit. Auch die schon angesprochenen Bestimmungen zur Wehrpflicht, zum Ersatzdienst und zu sonstigen Dienstleistungsverpflichtungen für Männer und Frauen im Verteidigungsfall (Art. 12a) fanden nun Eingang in die Verfassung.

- Nicht weniger als elf hinzufügte Artikel (115a-l), die im neuen Abschnitt X a zusammengefasst wurden, dienten darüber hinaus einer umfassenden Regelung der Verfassungsordnung im Verteidigungsfall. Für das bundesdeutsche Institutionensystem besonders bedeutsam waren der für diesen Fall festgeschriebene Übergang der militärischen Befehlsgewalt vom Verteidigungsminister auf den Kanzler (115b), die Überführung ausschließlicher Landeskompetenzen in den Katalog konkurrierender Gesetzgebung (115c), die Verlängerung von Amtszeiten bzw. Wahlperioden der Verfassungsorgane bis sechs Monate nach Ende des Verteidigungsfalls (115h) und die Möglichkeit beschleunigter Gesetzgebungsverfahren (115d).

Obwohl diese Bestimmungen bis heute glücklicherweise nicht zur Anwendung gekommen sind, schaffen sie ein alternatives Institutionenszenario für den Krisen- und insbesondere für den Verteidigungsfall, welches die Wehrhaftigkeit der grundgesetzlichen Ordnung besonders hervorkehrt und verdeutlicht, dass auch pluralistische Demokratien nicht davor zurückschrecken müssen, ihren Bestand mit effektiven Mitteln zu sichern.

7.4 Die Grundgesetzreform von 1994

Schon seit 1949 war in Artikel 146 die Möglichkeit vorgesehen, das Grundgesetz durch eine neue Verfassung abzulösen, „die von dem deutschen Volk in freier Entscheidung beschlossen worden ist". Bis zur Wende 1989 spielte dieser Passus keine praktische Rolle, da eine Wiedervereinigung des Landes als Basis für eine derartige konstitutionelle Fundamentalrevision bloße Utopie darstellte.

Und selbst als die Mauer gefallen war und sich nun dafür eine Chance geboten hätte, legten sich beide deutschen Regierungen im Einklang mit der Bevölkerungsmehrheit zügig auf einen Beitritt Ostdeutschlands zum Bundesgebiet gemäß Artikel 23 des Grundgesetzes ohne vorherige Schaffung einer neuen gesamtdeutschen Verfassung fest, da dies ein wesentlich einfacheres Verfahren zur Wiedervereinigung darstellte. Verschiedene alternative Verfassungsentwürfe (Runder Tisch, Kuratorium für einen demokratisch verfassten Bund deutscher Länder) wurden weitgehend ignoriert. Jedoch nahm man die Wiedervereinigung zum Anlass, wenigstens im Nachhinein über eine fundamentale Reform des Grundgesetzes nachzudenken, die dem Geist des Artikels 146 Rechnung trug.

Artikel 5 des Einigungsvertrags von 1990 trug daher dem Gesetzgeber in Form einer Empfehlung auf, „sich innerhalb von zwei Jahren mit den im Zusammenhang mit der deutschen Einigung aufgeworfenen Fragen zur Änderung oder Ergänzung des Grundgesetzes zu befassen". Insbesondere das „Verhältnis zwischen Bund und Ländern" sollte überprüft werden, wie auch die Liste der Staatszielbestimmungen. Zudem wurde eine spezielle Neugliederungsregelung für die Bundesländer Berlin und Brandenburg angeregt, und schließlich solle man sich „mit der Frage der Anwendung des Artikels 146 des Grundgesetzes und in deren Rahmen einer Volksabstimmung" genauer beschäftigen.

Die 1991 eingesetzte Gemeinsame Verfassungskommission, die von 64 Bundestags- und Bundesratsmitgliedern gebildet wurde, bekam den Auftrag, entsprechende Grundgesetzänderungen auszuarbeiten, die auch durch den Maastrichter Vertrag erforderlich geworden waren. Da für Kommissionsentscheidungen jeweils Zweidrittelmehrheiten nötig waren, setzte dies ein hohes Maß an Konsensbereitschaft voraus, begrenzte letztlich aber auch die Reichweite der Reformen. Die auf den Vorschlägen des Gremiums fußende Verfassungsrevision des Jahres 1994 umfasste schließlich folgende Bereiche:

- Mehrere neue Staatszielbestimmungen fanden nun Eingang in das Grundgesetz: Der Schutz der natürlichen Lebensgrundlagen (Art. 20a), die Gleichstellung Behinderter (Art. 3 Abs. (3)) sowie die staatliche Förderung der Durchsetzung geschlechtlicher Gleichberechtigung (Art. 3 Abs. (2)) sind seither integraler Bestandteil unseres Grundgesetzes. Der neugefasste Artikel 23 Abs. (1) gibt dem Bund zudem den Auftrag zur „Entwicklung der Europäischen Union", um die „Verwirklichung eines vereinten Europas" zu erreichen – dies aber nur unter Wahrung föderativer Grundsätze und des Prinzips der Subsidiarität: die deutsche Souveränität und Eigenstaatlichkeit sind verfassungsrechtlich also weiter unantastbar.

- Eine Neubestimmung des Bund-Länder-Verhältnisses wurde insbesondere durch Reformmaßnahmen im Bereich der Konkurrierenden Gesetzgebung versucht. Unter anderem sieht nun Abs. (4) des Artikels 72 grundsätzlich vor, „dass eine bundesgesetzliche Regelung, für die eine Erforderlichkeit ... nicht mehr besteht, durch Landesrecht ersetzt werden kann".

Noch längere Zeit ist dieser Passus jedoch 'Verfassungslyrik' geblieben, da ein Konsens aller sechzehn Länder über entsprechende Kompetenzübertragungen überaus schwer zu erzielen war. Denn sie sind durchweg mit vermehrten finanziellen Aufwendungen der Bundesländer für die wiedergewonnenen Aufgaben verbunden, was gerade nicht im Interesse der finanzschwachen Gliedstaaten liegt. Erst die Föderalismusreform I von 2006 konnte hier einen Durchbruch erzielen.

- Weiterhin wurde dem Wunsch nach einer Sonderregelung für die Länderneugliederung Berlins und Brandenburgs entsprochen. Der neu eingefügte Artikel 118a ermöglicht diese nun „abweichend von den Vorschriften des Artikels 29 unter Beteiligung ihrer Wahlberechtigten durch Vereinbarung beider Länder". Trotz der somit gesenkten verfassungsrechtlichen Hürden scheiterte aber ein erster Anlauf zur Vereinigung beider Länder im Jahre 1996, als die brandenburgische Bevölkerung das Projekt nach bereits erfolgter Billigung durch beide Landesparlamente sowie dem positiven Berliner Referendum durch ihr Veto doch noch stoppte. Bis heute jedoch ist ein neuer Anlauf in der Diskussion.

Letztlich war aber klar, dass die 1994 erfolgte „Verfassungsreform" ihren Namen eigentlich nicht verdiente. Zu marginal waren die erreichten Veränderungen, als dass das Grundgesetz eine neue Qualität erhalten hätte. Kritisiert wurde insbesondere die Nichtaufnahme plebiszitärer Entscheidungsverfahren, welche der Bevölkerung über Volksbegehren oder Referenden direkten Einfluss auf die bundesdeutsche Gesetzgebung ermöglicht hätten. Auch die Stärkung der gesetzgeberischen Zuständigkeiten der Landtage durch entsprechende Präzisierungen des Katalogs konkurrierender Gesetzgebung wurde von vielen schmerzlich vermisst und erst mit der Föderalismusreform I von 2006 entschiedener angegangen.

Viele Kritiker waren sich daher einig, dass dem Auftrag des Einigungsvertrages nach einer verfassungsrechtlichen Grundsatzreform nicht Rechnung getragen worden war. Freilich hielt man dem entgegen, dass die vergleichsweise geringen Änderungen der grundgesetzlichen Ordnung ja gerade als Qualitätsausweis der bisherigen, bewährten Verfassung zu werten seien, die deshalb ohne große Änderungen auch für das wiedervereinigte Gesamtdeutschland tauge. Und trotzdem entstand bei vielen Zeitgenossen das Gefühl, Zeugen eines verfassungspolitischen Immobilismus geworden zu sein.

7.5 Die Föderalismusreformen I und II

Nicht zuletzt deshalb wurde bald nach der Jahrtausendwende ein neuer Versuch unternommen, den deutschen Bundestaat grundlegend zu reformieren und insbesondere die Unitarisierung zulasten der Länder zu stoppen. Bundestag und Bundesrat setzten deshalb im Herbst 2003 eine gemeinsame „Kommission (…) zur Modernisierung der bundesstaatlichen Ordnung" ein.

Diese Föderalismuskommission erarbeitete unter den beiden Vorsitzenden Edmund Stoiber und Franz Müntefering ein umfassendes Reformpaket, das jedoch wegen unüberbrückbarer Differenzen auf dem Gebiet der Bildungspolitik Ende 2004 scheiterte. Aufgrund der von Kanzler Schröder auf das Jahr 2005 vorgezogenen Bundestagswahlen konnte das Projekt zudem wegen der verkürzten Legislaturperiode des Bundestages nicht wirkungsvoll weiterverfolgt werden.

Nach Bildung der Großen Koalition im Jahre 2005 gestalteten sich die Rahmenbedingungen jedoch wesentlich günstiger, zumal parteiübergreifend die Meinung vorherrschte, die guten Ansätze der Föderalismuskommission nun zügig zu einem guten Ende bringen zu können. Im Koalitionsvertrag der neuen Bundesregierung wurden daher deren Vorschläge über weite Strecken aufgegriffen und nach zügigen Beratungen in Bundestag und Bundesrat bereits im Herbst 2006 durch ein entsprechendes Paket von Grundgesetz- und einzelgesetzlichen Änderungen verwirklicht. Komplettiert wurde dies durch die Föderalismusreform II von 2009 mit umfassenden Bestimmungen zur Finanzverfassung.

Nicht alle dort geregelten Materien sind für die hier interessierende Institutionenordnung von Belang. Von zentraler Bedeutung jedoch wurden die Bestimmungen zur Neujustierung der Gesetzgebungskompetenzen zwischen Bund und Ländern. Zusammengefasst betrifft das insbesondere folgende Punkte:

- Ein Kernstück der Reform war in dieser Hinsicht zweifellos die Abschaffung der *Rahmengesetzgebung* des Bundes durch die ersatzlose Streichung des Grundgesetzartikels 75. Denn nicht zu Unrecht hatten Kritiker den politischen Unitarisierungstrend gerade an diesem legislativen Instrument festgemacht: Die Rahmengesetze des Bundes waren ihrem Namen gemäß ursprünglich als Instrument zur Festschreibung allgemeiner Grundsätze eingeführt worden, die den Ländern bei der konkreten Ausgestaltung viel Spielraum lassen sollten. De facto jedoch wurden sie im Laufe der Zeit immer detaillierter, wodurch die legislativen Ausgestaltungsmöglichkeiten der Länder hier immer geringer wurden. Kein Wunder also, dass gerade sie an einer konsequenten Reform dieses Missstands interessiert waren. Sinngemäß gilt das auch für die Änderung des Artikels 84 Abs. (1), durch den die Kommunen jetzt vor nicht gegenfinanzierten

Aufgabenübertragungen durch den Bund geschützt sind.

- Eine zweite wesentliche Maßnahme bestand in der deutlichen Einschränkung der *Zustimmungspflicht* des Bundesrats im Bereich der Bundesgesetzgebung, was nun wiederum der zentralstaatlichen Ebene zugutekam. Durch eine entsprechende Reform von Artikel 84 Abs. (1) wurde diese für die Fälle aufgehoben, wo die Verwaltungsverfahren in den Ländern durch Bundesgesetze tangiert waren. Stattdessen wurde diesen zugestanden, für deren Durchführung gegebenenfalls differierende Regelungen zu treffen. Und in der Folge reduzierte sich der Anteil zustimmungspflichtiger Gesetze in der Tat nicht unwesentlich.

- In etlichen Legislativbereichen wurde zudem der Gewichtszunahme des Bundes durch die wieder *deutlichere Trennung der Zuständigkeitsbereiche* entgegengewirkt: Insbesondere im Beamten- und im Strafvollzugs- sowie im Presse- und Versammlungsrecht sind nunmehr die Länder federführend. Das gilt auch für die Bildungspolitik, durch welche die traditionelle „Kulturhoheit der Länder" noch einmal gestärkt wurde: Die Gemeinschaftsaufgabe von Bund und Ländern im Hochschulbau wurde aus Artikel 91a gestrichen; dem Bund verbleiben am Ende nur magere Legislativkompetenzen im Bereich der Anerkennung von Hochschulabschlüssen und bei der Zulassung zum Studium. Auch die Bildungsplanung jenseits der Hochschulen obliegt den Ländern nun wieder selbst. Allerdings ist damit auch ein Rückzug des Bundes aus der Finanzierung dieser Bereiche verbunden, was gerade für schwächere Länder ein Problem darstellt und inzwischen zu entsprechenden Nachjustierungen geführt hat.

- Neben verschiedenen Erweiterungen der ausschließlichen Legislativkompetenz des Bundes (u.a. Kernenergie, Kriegsfolgenrecht, Meldewesen) ist in diesem Zusammenhang noch auf das neu geschaffene Instrument der *Abweichungsgesetzgebung* gemäß Artikel 72 Abs. (3) hinzuweisen: In nicht weniger als sechs Gesetzgebungsbereichen (Jagdwesen, Naturschutz- und Landschaftspflege, Bodenverteilung, Raumordnung, Wasserhaushalt, Hochschulzulassung und Hochschulabschlüsse) können die Bundesländer seither „durch Gesetz hiervon abweichende Regelungen treffen", wenn der Bund zuvor in diesem Bereich gesetzgeberisch tätig geworden ist. Auch dies wirkt einer Unitarisierung der gesamtdeutschen Rechtsordnung entgegen.

- Die Föderalismusreform II ergänzte dieses Maßnahmenpaket noch durch etliche *steuer- und haushaltsrechtliche Bestimmungen*: Von bestimmten Ausnahmen abgesehen sind Bund und Länder gemäß Artikel 109 Abs. (3) nunmehr gehalten, „die Haushalte (…) grundsätzlich ohne Einnahmen aus Krediten auszugleichen". Das soll einer kontinuierlichen Neuverschuldung durch laufende Kreditaufnahmen vorbeugen. Artikel 115 Abs. (2) präzisiert weiter: „Einnahmen und Ausgaben sind grundsätzlich ohne Einnahmen aus Krediten auszugleichen. Diesem Grundsatz ist entsprochen, wenn die Einnahmen aus Krediten 0,35 vom Hundert im Verhältnis zum nominalen Bruttoinlandsprodukt nicht überschreiten.“

Die Reformdiskussion wurde jedoch durch diese Maßnahmenpakete keineswegs schwächer, sondern schon bald erkannte Defizite fachten sie eher noch an. Zum einen wurde der neu geschaffenen Abweichungsgesetzgebung zugeschrieben, das deutsche Normensystem eher noch unübersichtlicher zu machen als den Ländern in ihrem Gestaltungswillen wirklich zu dienen. Zum anderen wurde schon bei der Verabschiedung der Föderalismusreform II angezweifelt, ob die strikten Maßnahmen zur Steuer- und Haushaltsdisziplin gerade für schwache Gebietskörperschaften wirklich praktikabel sind. Und so ist absehbar, dass auch dieses Reformprojekt eine Nachfolge finden wird.

8. Diskussionsschwerpunkte der Forschung

Die Institutionenordnung des Grundgesetzes hat seit ihrer Begründung im Jahre 1949 merkliche Änderungen erfahren. Sowohl punktuelle als auch umfassende Novellierungen der bundesdeutschen Verfassung trugen in der Summe dazu bei, dass die politische Entscheidungspraxis in Deutschland in vielerlei Hinsicht nicht mehr derjenigen der fünfziger und sechziger Jahre entspricht. Im Folgenden sollen abschließend die wesentlichen Problemkomplexe, die auch Gegenstand wissenschaftlicher Debatten und Kontroversen sind, schlaglichtartig thematisiert werden.

8.1 Machtverlust der Parlamente?

Schon in den sechziger Jahren diagnostizierte der streitbare Freiburger Politikwissenschaftler Wilhelm Hennis einen Trend zur Machterosion parlamentarischer Körperschaften. Auf Bundesebene verbuchte er eine Entwicklung zur exekutivlastigen Kanzlerdemokratie, deren „Regierungstechnik" auf eine Entparlamentarisierung des politischen Entscheidungsprozesses hinauslaufe. Wesentliche Projekte würden bereits im Apparat der Ministerialbürokratie vorgeprägt und durch die Regierung gleichsam im Eilverfahren durch das Parlament geschleust. Adenauers straffe Regierungspraxis, die auch durch einen kooperativen Bundesrat erleichtert wurde, ließ derartige Schlussfolgerungen durchaus plausibel erscheinen.

Darüber hinaus verwies Hennis auf den noch weiter reichenden Machtverlust der Länderparlamente, denen im Rahmen des immer bundeslastiger werdenden deutschen Föderalismus immer weniger eigene Gesetzgebungsbefugnisse zukämen und die zudem durch ihre eigenen Landesregierungen nach dem bundespolitischen Muster reglementiert würden. Der deutsche Parlamentarismus erleide deshalb gerade auf Länderebene einen zunehmenden Verlust an Legitimität, da die Volksvertretungen ihrer originären Funktion der Gesetzgebung nicht mehr nachkommen könnten.

Die nachfolgende Forschung hat dieses Bild deutlich modifiziert, zumal sich die „Macht der Parlamente" (Martin Sebaldt) im internationalen Vergleich ohnehin recht vielfältig und ohne klares Entwicklungsmuster darstellt. Zwar hielt auf Bundesebene der Trend zur Exekutivlastigkeit der Politik auch unter Adenauers Nachfolgern an. Jedoch zeigte sich spätestens mit dem Machtwechsel zur sozialliberalen Koalition im Jahre 1969, dass die reale Machtbasis des Bundestages sehr von den konkreten parteipolitischen Konstellationen abhing: Da die Bundesregierung zu diesem Zeitpunkt über keine Mehrheit befreundeter Landesregierungen im Bundesrat verfügte, stieg das parlamentarische Vetopotential der Unionsopposition gegenüber den Regierungen Brandt und Schmidt schlagartig an, was sich in einem ebenso deutlich gewachsenen parlamentarischen Einfluss auf die Bundesgesetzgebung niederschlug: So konnte ich nachweisen, dass nicht weniger als 20,2 Prozent aller in der 6. Wahlperiode (1969-1972) verabschiedeten Gesetze auf Oppositionsinitiativen aus dem Bundestag und dem Bundesrat zurückgingen!

Aber auch in früheren Legislaturperioden hatte die Bundestagsopposition hier schon entsprechende Erfolge verbuchen können, die allerdings nicht so spektakulär ausgefallen waren, als dass sie öffentlich wahrgenommen worden wären. Mit detaillierten empirischen Analysen der Bundesgesetzgebung der fünfziger und frühen sechziger Jahre konnte ich dafür ebenfalls konkrete Nachweise erbringen. Und auch für die frühen achtziger Jahre liegen ähnliche Befunde vor, welche die Rolle der Opposition als „anderer Beweger der Politik" (Carlo Schmid) belegen.

Unstrittiger ist dagegen bis heute die These vom Machtverlust der Länderparlamente, der durch den Trend zur *legislativen Unitarisierung* ebenfalls deutlich verstärkt worden ist. Fairerweise muss man dabei aber anmerken, dass den Bundesländern und damit auch ihren Parlamenten hier nicht zu einseitig die Rolle des Opfers zugeschrieben werden darf. Denn die dafür nötigen Grundgesetzänderungen waren immer auch mit den nötigen Zweidrittelmehrheiten des Bundesrates verabschiedet worden, wobei der Wunsch der Länder und ihrer Parlamente nach finanzieller Beteiligung des Bundes an Landesprojekten durchweg Pate stand. Somit trugen sie also selbst wesentlich zu dieser Unitarisierung bei. Es wird sich weisen, ob die Föderalismusreformen von

2006 und 2009 hier langfristig wirklich eine Trendwende einleiten und den Ausgangspunkt für die Rückübertragung von Bundeszuständigkeiten auf die Länder bilden werden.

8.2 Politikverflechtungsfalle?

Fritz Scharpf hat im Jahre 1985 in einem bereits klassisch gewordenen Aufsatz kein schmeichelhaftes Bild des deutschen Föderalismus gezeichnet: Er sei durch eine „Politikverflechtungsfalle" gekennzeichnet, die das bundesdeutsche Staatsgefüge unbeweglich und entscheidungsschwach mache: Die enge institutionelle Verflechtung von Bundes- und Landesebene eröffne zu viele Veto- und Blockadeoptionen, gerade für die im Bundesrat versammelten Landesregierungen, als dass bundespolitische Entscheidungen zügig gefällt und umgesetzt werden könnten.

Scharpfs Diagnose schloss an die schon länger existierende Kritik am deutschen Verbundföderalismus an, verlieh ihr aber durch die Systematik seiner Argumente neuen Nachdruck. Reformforderungen wurden immer lauter, die insbesondere eine Abschwächung des Verbundcharakters und eine deutlichere institutionelle und kompetenzmäßige Trennung zwischen der Bundes- und der Landesebene anregten. Gerade von Seiten der politischen Praxis wurde hier der duale US-amerikanische Föderalismus immer wieder als Vorbild in den Raum gestellt, wobei die auch dort zu beobachtenden

Unitarisierungs- und Politikverflechtungstendenzen oft geflissentlich übersehen wurden.

Auch Gerhard Lehmbruch diagnostizierte in seinem Klassiker „Parteienwettbewerb im Bundesstaat" entsprechende Reformblockaden. Er hatte erkannt, dass das gesamte föderale Entscheidungsgefüge Deutschlands durch eine bundespolitische Aufladung der Länderkammer entscheidend verändert worden war: Hatten die Verfassungsgeber von 1949 noch im Sinn, den Bundesrat zum *Vertretungsorgan originärer Länderinteressen* zu machen, die in *Verhandlungen* mit Bundestag und Bundesregierung zur Geltung gebracht werden sollten, mutierte die Länderkammer im Laufe der Jahrzehnte jedoch immer mehr zur zweiten bundespolitischen Arena, wo sich die einzelnen Ministerpräsidenten meist nicht nach ihrer regionalen, sondern nach ihrer *parteipolitischen* Zuordnung gegeneinander formierten.

Lehmbruch diagnostizierte damit zu Recht ein 'Überschwappen' des bundespolitischen „Parteienwettbewerbs" auf den Bundesrat zulasten regionaler Interessenvertretung und verhandlungsdemokratischer Entscheidungssuche zwischen Bund und Ländern. Auch auf Politik und Wahlkämpfe in den einzelnen Ländern begann die Bundespolitik nun immer größeren Einfluss auszuüben, indem zunehmend nationale Themen dort die Agenda bestimmten.

Jedoch hat die empirische Forschung auch hier zu einer deutlichen Modifikation des Bildes beigetragen. Denn zum einen ließ die Analyse der Bundesgesetzgebung keinen Zweifel daran aufkommen, dass der Bundesrat seine Vetomacht letztlich nur behutsam ausübte und nur punktuell Projekte völlig blockierte: Von 9256 Gesetzesvorlagen der 1.-14. Wahlperiode (1949-2002) versagte die Länderkammer im ersten Beratungsdurchgang lediglich 150 die Zustimmung. Nach anschließenden Vermittlungsverfahren konnte bei weiteren 84 von ihnen Einigung zwischen Bundestag und Bundesrat erzielt werden. Und so blieben am Ende lediglich 66 Vorlagen übrig, die am Einspruch der Länderkammer gänzlich scheiterten.

Eine gleichmäßige parteipolitische Polarisierung in und zwischen beiden Kammern ist also hieran nicht ablesbar, und dies auch nicht bei abweichenden Bundestags- und Bundesratsmehrheiten. Dazu gesagt sei jedoch, dass das Vetopotential des Bundesrates wesentlich häufiger für die *informelle* Erzwingung substantieller Änderungen in Regierungsvorlagen eingesetzt wurde, was in dieser Pauschalstatistik so nicht zum Ausdruck kommt. Aber auch dies belegt ein ausgeprägtes kammerübergreifendes Konsenspotential.

Zudem vermochte gerade das gescholtene deutsche Parteiensystem drohende institutionelle Blockaden meist zu verhindern, indem es die Vorkonzertierung von Bundes- und Landespolitik wesentlich beförderte. Wolfgang Renzsch hat darauf hingewiesen, dass politische Vorabsprachen von Bundesregierung und Länderregierungen der eigenen Couleur immer mehr im Rahmen von Parteigremien der eigenen Bundespartei erfolgen. Gerade in Zeiten gleichartiger Mehrheitsverhältnisse in Bundestag und Bundesrat beschleunigt dies den bundespolitischen Entscheidungsgang erheblich und führt zu einer nochmaligen Reduzierung des ohnehin schon moderat gestalteten Vetoverhaltens der Länderkammer. Parteien können dann erfolgreich als 'Schmiermittel' fungieren.

In Zeiten divergierender Mehrheiten ist dieser Mechanismus allerdings Störungen unterworfen, und zudem ist er gerade durch die Pluralisierung des deutschen Parteiensystems seit der deutschen Wiedervereinigung immer schwerer zu kalkulieren: Denn die Koalitionsformate der Landesregierungen werden dadurch immer zahlreicher, und die früher relativ einfache Rechnung, ob eine Landesregierung nun in Opposition zum Bund stehe oder nicht, ist angesichts wachsender parteilicher Überschneidungen zwischen den Koalitionen heute immer schwieriger.

8.3 Immobilismus im Mehrebenensystem?

Die fortschreitende europäische Integration hat die Verflechtung der politischen Ebenen noch einmal komplexer gemacht. In Fortführung seiner Argumentation vertrat Fritz Scharpf die These, die Politikverflechtungsfalle sei durch den weitreichenden Vergemeinschaftungsprozess verschiedenster Politikfelder noch wesentlich bedrohlicher geworden: Denn zusätzlich zu den klassischen Bund-Länder-Problemen wüchsen nun die Abstimmungserfordernisse und gegenseitigen Blockadepotentiale zwischen den EU-Gemeinschaftsorganen und den anderen Mitgliedstaaten einerseits und dem deutschen Bundesstaat andererseits.

Spätestens seit dem Maastrichter Vertrag im Jahre 1992 war dieser Sachverhalt am langen Katalog dort verankerter „Gemeinschaftspolitiken" der EU ablesbar: Nicht weniger als 21 von ihnen wurden dort allein im EG-Vertrag festgeschrieben, von der Agrar-, Wettbewerbs- und Handelspolitik über die Zusammenarbeit im Zollwesen und die Sozialpolitik bis zum Verbraucherschutz und der Bildungs- und Kulturpolitik reichend. Substantielle Kompetenzen der EU waren also bei fast jeder politischen Entscheidung immer mehr zu berücksichtigen und reicherten damit das 'traditionelle' Feld aus bundes- und landespolitischen 'Vetospielern' noch um die politischen Akteure der europäischen Ebene an.

Doch lauern noch weitere Probleme hinter dieser institutionellen Mehrebenenarchitektur. Denn bis heute wurden die Zuständigkeiten nur selten einer Entscheidungsebene zugeordnet, etwa in der Handels- und in der Zollpolitik, die als voll vergemeinschaftete Politikfelder auch voll in die Regelungskompetenz der EU fallen. Beim Löwenanteil der Gemeinschaftspolitiken ist dagegen gemäß dem Vertrag von Lissabon nur eine „geteilte Zuständigkeit" (u.a. für Binnenmarkt, Landwirtschaft, Umwelt, Verkehr, Energie, Verbraucherschutz) oder sogar nur eine koordinative Funktion (u.a. Bildung, Kultur, Gesundheit) der Gemeinschaft vorgesehen.

Gemäß Artikel 5 Abs. (3) EUV wird die EU hier infolgedessen nur tätig, „sofern und soweit die Ziele der in Betracht gezogenen Maßnahmen von den Mitgliedstaaten weder auf zentraler noch auf regionaler oder lokaler Ebene ausreichend verwirklicht werden können, sondern vielmehr wegen ihres Umfangs oder ihrer Wirkungen auf Unionsebene besser zu verwirklichen sind." Obwohl diese allgemeine Formulierung durch spätere Vertragszusätze weiter präzisiert wurde, lässt sie immer noch genügend Interpretationsspielraum.

Neben vielen anderen hat Edgar Grande daher auf die daraus resultierenden Entscheidungsdilemmata hingewiesen: Die letztlich unscharfe Kompetenzaufteilung verführt Mitgliedstaaten wie Gemeinschaftsorgane dazu, unbequeme Materien auf die jeweils andere Entscheidungsebene abzuschieben („cuckoo game") bzw. im Falle von Problemen die Schuld abzuwälzen („blame avoidance").

Schlagendes Beispiel hierfür war etwa das BSE-Problem rund um die Jahrtausendwende: Während Renate Künast, Agrar- und Verbraucherschutzministerin der rot-grünen Koalition, immer wieder auf Versäumnisse der EU verwies, die schon längst eine Richtlinie zum endgültigen Verbot von Tiermehlbeimengungen in Viehfutter hätte verabschieden müssen, wehrte sich der zuständige Agrarkommissar Fischler mit dem Argument, eine derartige Initiative sei in den letzten Jahren in erster Linie am deutschen Widerstand gescheitert.

Ein politischer Immobilismus könnte daher der europäischen und der deutschen Politik in Zukunft durchaus drohen. Nicht von ungefähr ist es daher gerade den Deutschen ein Anliegen, in der EU-Reformdiskussion auf eine deutlichere Kompetenztrennung zwischen den Entscheidungsebenen hinzuwirken: Schon in ihrem nationalen föderalen Gefüge schaffen vielfältige Kompetenzüberschneidungen zwischen Bund und Ländern genug Entscheidungsprobleme. Eine dauerhafte Verankerung derselben auch in der EU würde gerade unser Land vor besonders große Schwierigkeiten stellen.

Grundgesetzänderungen seit 1949

	Änderungsgesetz	In Kraft seit
1.	Strafrechtsänderungsgesetz (Art. 143): Aufhebung von Übergangsbestimmungen	31.08.51
2.	Ges. zur Einfügung eines Art. 120a in das GG: Lastenausgleich	18.08.52
3.	Ges. zur Änd. des Art. 107 des GG: Übergangsbestimmungen	23.04.53
4.	Ges. zur Erg. des GG (Art. 73, 79, 142a): Wehrverfassung; Pariser Verträge	28.03.54
5.	Zweites Ges. zur Änd. des Art. 107 des GG: Übergangsbestimmungen	31.12.54
6.	Ges. zur Änd. und Erg. der Finanzverfassung (Art. 106, 107): Finanzverfassung	01.04.55
7.	Ges. zur Erg. des Grundgesetzes (Art. 1, 12, 17a, 36, 45a, 45b, 49, 59a, 60, 65a, 87a, 87b, 96, 96a, 137, 143): Wehrverfassung	22.03.56
8.	Ges. zur Änd. und Erg. des Art. 106 des GG: Steuerverteilung	01.04.57/ 01.04.58
9.	Ges. zur Einfügung eines Art. 135a in das GG: Kriegsfolgelasten	27.10.57
10.	Ges. zur Erg. des GG (Art. 74, 87c): Kernenergie	01.01.60
11.	Ges. zur Einfügung eines Artikels über die Luftverkehrsverwaltung in das GG (Art. 87d)	16.02.61
12.	Zwölftes Ges. zur Änd. des GG (Art. 96, 96a): Bundesgerichte, Wehrstrafgerichte	12.03.61
13.	Dreizehntes Ges. zur Änd. des GG (Art. 74): Kriegsfolgelasten	27.06.65
14.	Vierzehntes Ges. zur Änd. des GG (Art. 120): Kriegsfolgelasten	05.08.65

15.	Fünfzehntes Ges. zur Änd. des GG (Art. 109): Gesamtwirtschaftliches Gleichgewicht	14.06.67
16.	Sechzehntes Ges. zur Änd. des GG (Art. 92, 95, 96, 96a, 99, 100): Reform Bundesgerichte	23.06.68
17.	Siebzehntes Ges. zur Erg. des GG (Art. 9, 10, 11, 12, 12a, 19, 20, 35, 53a, 59a, 65a, 73, 80a, 87a, 91, 115a-l, 142a, 143): Notstand, Verteid.	28.06.68
18	Achtzehntes Ges. zur Änd. des GG (Art. 76, 77): Fristen für Gesetzvorlagen	20.11.68
19.	Neunzehntes Ges. zur Änd. des GG (Art. 93, 94): Verfassungsbeschwerden	02.02.69
20.	Zwanzigstes Ges. zur Änd. des GG (Art. 109, 110, 112, 113, 114, 115): Haushaltsrecht	15.05.69
21.	Einundzwanzigstes Ges. zur Änd. des GG (Art. 91a, 91b, 104a, 105, 106, 107, 108, 115c, 115k): Finanzverfassung, Gemeinschaftsaufg.	01.01.70
22.	Zweiundzwanzigstes Ges. zur Änd. des GG (Art. 74, 75, 96): Gesetzgebung, Hochschulen	15.05.69
23.	Dreiundzwanzigstes Ges. zur Änd. des GG (Art. 76): Fristen für Gesetzesvorlagen	23.07.69
24.	Vierundzwanzigstes Ges. zur Änd. des GG (Art. 120): Kriegsfolgelasten	01.08.69
25.	Fünfundzwanzigstes Ges. zur Änd. des GG (Art. 29): Neugliederung des Bundesgebietes	23.08.69
26.	Sechsundzwanzigstes Ges. zur Änd. des GG (Art. 96): Gerichtsbarkeit im Staatsschutz	30.08.69
27.	Siebenundzwanzigstes Ges. zur Änd. des GG (Art. 38, 91a): Wahlalter, Hochschulbau	06.08.70
28.	Achtundzwanzigstes Ges. zur Änd. des GG (Art. 74a, 75, 98): Öffentlicher Dienst	21.03 71
29.	Neunundzwanzigstes Ges. zur Änd. des GG (Art. 74): Tierschutz	21.03 71
30.	Dreißigstes Ges. zur Änd. des GG (Art. 74): Umweltschutz	15.04 72
31.	Einunddreißigstes Ges. zur Änd. des GG (Art. 35, 73, 74, 87): Strafverfolgung durch Bund	03.08.72

32.	Zweiunddreißigstes Ges. zur Änd. des GG (Art. 45c): Petitionsausschuss	19.07.75
33.	Dreiunddreißigstes Ges. zur Änd. des GG (Art. 29, 39, 45, 45a, 49): Neugliederung Bundesgebiet, Wahlperiode	28.08.76/ 14.12.76
34.	Vierunddreißigstes Ges. zur Änd. des GG (Art. 74: Sprengstoffrecht	28.08.76
35.	Fünfunddreißigstes Ges. zur Änd. des GG (Art. 21): Parteivermögen	01.01.84
36.	Einigungsvertragsgesetz (Präambel, 23, 51, 135a, 143, 146): Deutsche Einheit, Stimmenverteilung im Bundesrat, Bestimmungen für Beitrittsgebiet	29.09.90
37.	Ges. zur Änd. des GG (Art. 87d): Luftverkehrsverwaltung	22.07.92
38.	Ges. zur Änd. des GG (Art. 23, 24, 28, 45, 50, 52, 88, 115e): Europäische Union (Maastricht)	25.12.92
39.	Ges. zur Änd. des GG (Art. 16, 16a, 18): Asylrecht	30.06.93
40.	Ges. zur Änd. des GG (Art. 73, 74, 80, 87, 87e, 106, 143a): Bahnstrukturreform	23.12.93
41.	Ges. zur Änd. des GG (Art. 73, 80, 87, 87f, 143b): Postneuordnung	03.09.94
42.	Ges. zur Änd. des GG (Art. 3, 20a, 28, 29, 72, 74, 75, 76, 77, 80, 87, 93, 118a, 125a): Staatsziele, Neugliederung Bundesgebiet, Gesetzgebung	15.11.94
43.	Ges. zur Änd. des GG (Art. 106): Lastenverteilung zwischen Bund und Ländern	11.11.95
44.	Ges. zur Änd. des GG (Art. 28, 106): Umsatzsteuer	25.10.97
45.	Ges. zur Änd. des GG (Art. 13): Akustische Überwachung	01.04.98
46.	Ges. zur Änd. des GG (Art. 39): Bundestagswahlperiode	27.10.98
47.	Ges. zur Änd. des GG (Art. 16): Auslieferung Deutscher an EU-Staaten und intern. Gerichte	02.12.00

48.	Ges. zur Änd. des GG (Art. 12a): Freiwilliger Waffendienst von Frauen	23.12.00
49.	Ges. zur Änd. des GG (Art. 108): Aufbau von Steuerbehörden	30.11.01
50.	Ges. zur Änd. des GG (Art. 20a): Staatsziel Tierschutz	01.08.02
51.	Ges. zur Änd. des GG (Art. 96): Gerichtszuständigkeiten im Völkerstrafrecht	01.08.02
52.	Ges. zur Änderung des GG (Art. 22, 23, 33, 52, 72, 73, 74, 74a, 75, 84, 85, 87c, 91a, 91b, 93, 98, 104a, 104b, 105, 107, 109, 125a, 125b, 125c, 143c): Modernisierung des Bundesstaats	01.09.06
53.	Ges. zur Änderung des GG (Art. 23, 45, 93): Rechte nationaler Parlamente in der EU, Abstrakte Normenkontrolle durch Bundestag	04.12.09
54.	Ges. zur Änderung des GG (Art. 106, 106b, 107, 108): KfZ-Steuer	01.07.09
55.	Ges. zur Änderung des GG (Art. 45d): Parl. Kontrollgremium des Bundestages	23.07.09
56.	Ges. zur Änderung des GG (Art. 87d): Einheitlicher Europäischer Luftraum	01.08.09
57.	Ges. zur Änderung des GG (Art. 91c, 91d, 104b, 109, 109a, 115, 143d): Finanzverfassung	01.08.09
58.	Ges. zur Änderung des GG (Art. 91e): Zuständigkeit für die Grundsicherung Arbeitssuchender	27.07.10
59.	Ges. zur Änderung des GG (Art. 93): Anerkennungsverfahren für politische Parteien	17.07.12
60.	Ges. zur Änderung des GG (Art. 91b): Forschungsförderung durch den Bund	01.01.15
Quelle: Datenhandbücher Bundestag 1949-1999, Kap. 14.2, 1990-2010, Kap. 13.2; eigene Ergänzungen.		

Auswahlbibliographie

Andersen, Uwe/ Wichard Woyke (Hg.), 2013: Handwörterbuch des politischen Systems der Bundesrepublik Deutschland, 7. Aufl., Wiesbaden.

Bauer, Angela/ Mathias Jestaedt, 1997: Das Grundgesetz im Wortlaut. Änderungsgesetze, Synopse, Textstufen und Vokabular zum Grundgesetz, Heidelberg.

Bergius, Michael, 2002: Im Bremser-Häuschen möchte Fischler nicht sitzen. EU-Kommissar sieht reichlich Spielraum für die von Künast proklamierte Agrarwende, in: Frankfurter Rundschau, 15.01., S. 9.

Beyme, Klaus von, 1997: Der Gesetzgeber. Der Bundestag als Entscheidungszentrum, Opladen.

Beyme, Klaus von, 1999: Das politische System der Bundesrepublik Deutschland, 9. Aufl., München.

Bieber, Roland u.a., 2011: Die Europäische Union. Europarecht und Politik, 9. Aufl., Baden-Baden.

Billing, Werner, 2001: Der Bundespräsident, in: Raban Graf von Westphalen (Hg.): Deutsches Regierungssystem. München, Wien, S. 313-337.

Born, Karl Erich, 1982: Von der Reichsgründung bis zum Ersten Weltkrieg, 7. Aufl., München.

Datenhandbuch zur Geschichte des Deutschen Bundestages 1949 bis 1990 (Autor: Peter Schindler), 1999: Gesamtausgabe in drei Bänden, Baden Baden.

Datenhandbuch zur Geschichte des Deutschen Bundestages 1990 bis 2010 (Autor: Michael F. Feldkamp), 2011: Gesamtausgabe in drei Bänden, Baden Baden.

Decker, Frank/ Viola Neu (Hg.), 2013: Handbuch der deutschen Parteien, 2. Aufl., Wiesbaden.

Detjen, Joachim, 2012: Verfassungswerte. Welche Werte bestimmen das Grundgesetz?, Bonn.

Doering-Manteuffel, Anselm, 1983: Die Bundesrepublik Deutschland in der Ära Adenauer. Außenpolitik und innere Entwicklung 1949-1963, Darmstadt.

Durth, K. Rüdiger, 2002: Verpasste Sternstunde. Der Politkrimi vor und hinter den Kulissen, in: Das Parlament 52, Nr. 13-14.

Ebert, Thomas, 2015: Soziale Gerechtigkeit. Ideen, Geschichte, Kontroversen, 2. Aufl., Bonn.

Egle, Christoph u.a. (Hg.), 2003: Das rot-grüne Projekt. Eine Bilanz der Regierung Schröder 1998-2002, Wiesbaden.

Egle, Christoph/ Reimut Zohlnhöfer (Hg.), 2007: Ende des rot-grünen Projektes. Eine Bilanz der Regierung Schröder 2002-2005, Wiesbaden.

Egle, Christoph/ Reimut Zohlnhöfer (Hg.), 2010: Die zweite Große Koalition. Eine Bilanz der Regierung Merkel 2005-2009, Wiesbaden.

Fenske, Hans, 2001: Der moderne Verfassungsstaat. Eine vergleichende Geschichte von der Entstehung bis zum 20. Jahrhundert, Paderborn et al.

Fischer Chronik Deutschland, 1999: Die Fischer Chronik Deutschland 1949-1999, Frankfurt a.M.

Friedrich, Manfred, 1986: Verfassung, in: Wolfgang W. Mickel (Hg.) in Verbindung mit Dietrich Zitzlaff: Handlexikon zur Politikwissenschaft, Bonn, S. 542-545.

Gast, Henrik, 2011: Der Bundeskanzler als politischer Führer. Potenziale und Probleme deutscher Regierungschefs aus interdisziplinärer Perspektive, Wiesbaden.

Gerlach, Irene, 1999: Bundesrepublik Deutschland. Entwicklung, Strukturen und Akteure eines politischen Systems. Mit CD: Dokumente und Quellen, Opladen.

Grande, Edgar, 2000: Multi-Level Governance: Institutionelle Besonderheiten und Funktionsbedingungen des europäischen Mehrebenensystems, in: Edgar Grande/ Markus Jachtenfuchs (Hg.), Wie problemlösungsfähig ist die EU? Regieren im europäischen Mehrebenensystem, Baden-Baden, S. 11-30.

Gündisch, Jürgen/ Mathijsen, Petrus, 1999: Rechtsetzung und Interessenvertretung in der Europäischen Union. Verfahren, Mitwirkung, Qualität, Legitimation, Stuttgart u.a.

Hamm-Brücher, Hildegard, 1990: Der freie Volksvertreter –
eine Legende? Erfahrungen mit parlamentarischer Macht
und Ohnmacht, München.

Hartmann, Jürgen/ Udo Kempf, 2011: Staatsoberhäupter in
der Demokratie, Wiesbaden.

Helms, Ludger, 1998: Keeping Weimar at Bay: The Federal
Presidency since 1949, in: German Politics and Society 16,
S. 50-68.

Helms, Ludger, 2000a: Introduction: Institutional Change and
Adaptation in a Stable Democracy, in: ders. (Hg.): Institu-
tions and Institutional Change in the Federal Republic of
Germany, Basingstoke et al., S. 1-31.

Helms, Ludger, 2000b: The Federal Constitutional Court: In-
stitutionalising Judicial Review in a Semisovereign Democracy, in: Ludger Helms (Hg.): Institutions and Institutional
Change in the Federal Republic of Germany, Basingstoke
et al., S. 84-104.

Hennis, Wilhelm, 1964: Richtlinienkompetenz und Regierungstechnik (Recht und Staat in Geschichte und Gegenwart, Bd.300/301), Tübingen.

Hennis, Wilhelm, 1976: Parlamentarische Opposition und In-
dustriegesellschaft. Zur Lage des parlamentarischen Regie-
rungssystems, in: Hans-Gerd Schumann (Hg.): Die Rolle
der Opposition in der Bundesrepublik Deutschland. Darmstadt, S. 88-113 (erstm. 1956).

Hesse, Joachim Jens/ Thomas Ellwein, 2012: Das Regierungssystem der Bundesrepublik Deutschland, 10. Aufl., Baden-
Baden.

Hesselberger, Dieter, 2003: Das Grundgesetz. Kommentar für
die politische Bildung, Bonn.

Hidalgo, Oliver, 2014: Die Antinomien der Demokratie,
Frankfurt a.M., New York.

Hirscher, Gerhard/ Karl-Rudolf Korte (Hg.), 2001: Aufstieg
und Fall von Regierungen. Machterwerb und Machterosio-
nen in westlichen Demokratien, München.

Hübner, Emil, 2000: Parlament und Regierung in der Bundesrepublik Deutschland, 2. Aufl., München.

Huhn, Jochen, 1992: Die Aktualität der Geschichte. Die west-deutsche Föderalismusdiskussion, in: Jochen Huhn/ Peter Christian Witt (Hg.): Föderalismus in Deutschland. Tradition und gegenwärtige Probleme, Baden-Baden, S. 31-53.

Ismayr, Wolfgang, 2009: Das politische System Deutschlands, in: Wolfgang Ismayr (Hg.) unter Mitarb. von Jörg Bonnefeld und Stephan Fischer: Die politischen Systeme Westeuropas, 4. Aufl., Wiesbaden, S. 515-565.

Ismayr, Wolfgang, 2012: Der Deutsche Bundestag im politischen System der Bundesrepublik Deutschland, 3. Aufl., Opladen.

Jäger, Wolfgang, 1998: Der Präsident, in: Wolfgang Jäger/ Wolfgang Welz (Hg.): Regierungssystem der USA. Lehr und Handbuch, 2. Aufl. München, Wien, S. 136-169.

Kaldrak, Gerd, 1982: Soldat und Politik: Der Umgang mit Politik – ein Problem für Soldaten, in: Peter Barth (Hg.): Die Bundeswehr in Staat und Gesellschaft, München, S 77-112.

Kempf, Udo, 2017: Das politische System Frankreichs, 5. akt. Aufl., Wiesbaden.

Kielmansegg, Peter Graf, 2013: Die Grammatik der Freiheit. Acht Versuche über den demokratischen Verfassungsstaat, Bonn.

Kilper, Heiderose/ Roland Lhotta, 1996: Föderalismus in der Bundesrepublik Deutschland. Eine Einführung, Opladen.

Kleßmann, Christoph, 1988: Zwei Staaten, eine Nation. Deutsche Geschichte 1955-1970, Bonn.

Kluxen, Kurt, 1983: Geschichte und Problematik des Parlamentarismus, Frankfurt a. M.

Kneuer, Marianne (Hg.), 2015: Standortbestimmung Deutschlands: Innere Verfasstheit und internationale Verantwortung, Baden-Baden.

Korte, Karl-Rudolf/ Manuel Fröhlich, 2004: Politik und Regieren in Deutschland. Strukturen, Prozesse, Entscheidungen, Paderborn u.a.

Kranenpohl, Uwe, 2010: Hinter dem Schleier des Beratungsgeheimnisses. Der Willensbildungs- und Entscheidungsprozess des Bundesverfassungsgerichts, Wiesbaden.

Landfried, Christine, 1984: Bundesverfassungsgericht und Gesetzgeber, Baden-Baden.

Laufer, Heinz/ Ursula Münch, 2010: Das föderale System der Bundesrepublik Deutschland, 8. Aufl., München.

Lehmann, Hans Georg, 1995: Deutschland-Chronik 1945 bis 1995, Bonn.

Lehmbruch, Gerhard, 2000: Parteienwettbewerb im Bundesstaat, 3. Aufl., Wiesbaden.

Leiße, Olaf (Hg.), 2010: Die Europäische Union nach dem Vertrag von Lissabon, Wiesbaden.

Lhotta, Roland, 2002: Konsens und Konkurrenz in der konstitutionellen Ökonomie bikameraler Verhandlungsdemokratie: Der Vermittlungsausschuss als effiziente Institution politischer Deliberation, in: Oberreuter/ Kranenpohl/ Sebaldt (Hg.): Der Deutsche Bundestag im Wandel, a.a.O., S. 93-117.

Linsenmann, Ingo, 2002: Europäische Zentralbank, in: Werner Weidenfeld/ Wolfgang Wessels (Hg.): Europa von A bis Z. Taschenbuch der europäischen Integration, 8. Aufl., Bonn, S. 176-178.

Löw, Konrad, 1995: Der Staat des Grundgesetzes, München.

Niclauß, Karlheinz, 1988: Kanzlerdemokratie. Bonner Regierungspraxis von Konrad Adenauer bis Helmut Kohl, Stuttgart et al.

Nohlen, Dieter, 2007: Wahlrecht und Parteiensystem. Zur Theorie und Empirie der Wahlsysteme, 5., überarb. und erw. Aufl., Opladen, Farmington Hills.

Oberreuter, Heinrich, 1978: Notstand und Demokratie. Vom monarchischen Obrigkeits- zum demokratischen Rechtsstaat, München.

Oberreuter, Heinrich, 1989: Von der Kapitulation zur Gründung der Bundesrepublik, in: Heinrich Oberreuter: Bewährung und Herausforderung. Zum Verfassungsverständnis der Bundesrepublik Deutschland, München, S. 11-31.

Oberreuter, Heinrich u.a., 2000: Die politischen Parteien in Deutschland. Geschichte, Programmatik, Organisation, Finanzierung, 26. aktual. Aufl., München.

Oberreuter, Heinrich, 2012: Republikanische Demokratie. Der Verfassungsstaat im Wandel, Baden-Baden.

Heinrich Oberreuter/Uwe Kranenpohl/Martin Sebaldt (Hg.), 2002: Der Deutsche Bundestag im Wandel. Ergebnisse neuerer Parlamentarismusforschung, 2., durchges. und erw. Aufl., Wiesbaden.

Patzelt, Werner J., 1995: Abgeordnete und ihr Beruf. Interviews – Umfragen – Analysen. Mit einem Vorwort von Rita Süssmuth, Berlin.

Pfetsch, Frank R., 1990: Ursprünge der Zweiten Republik, Opladen.

Reinhard, Wolfgang, 2000: Geschichte der Staatsgewalt. Eine vergleichende Verfassungsgeschichte Europas von den Anfängen bis zur Gegenwart, München.

Renzsch, Wolfgang, 1998: Parteien im Bundesstaat. Sand oder Öl im Getriebe?, in: Ursula Männle (Hg.): Föderalismus zwischen Konsens und Konkurrenz: Tagungs- und Materialienband zur Fortentwicklung des deutschen Föderalismus, Baden-Baden, S. 93-100.

Rudzio, Wolfgang, 2000: The Federal Presidency: Parameters of Presidential Power in a Parliamentary Democracy, in: Ludger Helms (Hg.): Institutions and Institutional Change in the Federal Republic of Germany, Basingstoke u.a., S. 48-64.

Rudzio, Wolfgang, 2011: Das politische System der Bundesrepublik Deutschland, 8. Aufl., Wiesbaden.

Saalfeld, Thomas, 1998: Großbritannien. Eine politische Landeskunde, Berlin.

Säcker, Horst, 2008: Das Bundesverfassungsgericht, 7. Aufl., München.

Scharpf, Fritz W., 1985: Die Politikverflechtungsfalle: Europäische Integration und deutscher Föderalismus im Vergleich, in Politische Vierteljahresschrift 26, S. 323-356.

Schmid, Carlo, 1976: Die Opposition als Staatseinrichtung, in: Hans-Gerd Schumann (Hg.): Die Rolle der Opposition in der Bundesrepublik Deutschland (Wege der Forschung, Bd. 422), Darmstadt, S. 53-65 (erstm. 1955).

Schmidt, Manfred G., 2010: Das politische System Deutschlands. Institutionen, Willensbildung und Politikfelder, Bonn.

Schreyer, Bernhard/ Manfred Schwarzmeier, 2000: Grundkurs Politikwissenschaft: Studium der Politischen Systeme. Eine studienorientierte Einführung, Wiesbaden.

Schwarz, Hans-Peter (Koord.), 2008: Die Bundesrepublik Deutschland. Eine Bilanz nach 60 Jahren, München.

Sebaldt, Martin, 1992: Die Thematisierungsfunktion der Opposition. Die parlamentarische Minderheit des Deutschen Bundestags als innovative Kraft im politischen System der Bundesrepublik Deutschland, Frankfurt a.M. u.a.

Sebaldt, Martin, 2002b: Parlamentarismus im Zeitalter der Europäischen Integration. Zu Logik und Dynamik politischer Entscheidungsprozesse im demokratischen Mehrebenensystem der EU, Opladen.

Sebaldt, Martin, 2009: Die Macht der Parlamente. Funktionen und Leistungsprofile nationaler Volksvertretungen in den alten Demokratien der Welt, Wiesbaden.

Sebaldt, Martin, 2015: Pathologie der Demokratie. Defekte, Ursachen und Therapie des modernen Staates, Wiesbaden.

Shell, Kurt L., 1998: Der Oberste Gerichtshof, in: Wolfgang Jäger/ Wolfgang Welz (Hg.): Regierungssystem der USA. Lehr- und Handbuch, 2. Aufl. München, Wien, S. 170-182.

Sturm, Roland, 2001: Föderalismus in Deutschland, Opladen.

Sturm, Roland/ Heinrich Pehle, 2005: Das neue deutsche Regierungssystem, 2. Aufl., Wiesbaden.

Stüwe, Klaus, 2002: Das Bundesverfassungsgericht als Vetospieler: Der Erfolg oppositioneller Verfahrensinitiativen vor dem Bundesverfassungsgericht (1951-2000), in: Oberreuter/ Kranenpohl/ Sebaldt (Hg.): Der Deutsche Bundestag im Wandel, a.a.O., S. 145-167.

Thiel, Elke, 1997: Die Europäische Union, 5. Aufl., München.

Verträge zur Einheit Deutschlands, 1990: Die Verträge zur Einheit Deutschlands. Textausgabe mit Sachverzeichnis und einer Einführung von Ingo Münch, München.

Vertrag von Lissabon, 2010: Konsolidierte Fassung, Bonn.

Weber, Jürgen, 1981: Geschöpfe der Alliierten. Die Länder und ihre Zusammenarbeit, in: Jürgen Weber (Hg.): Auf dem Wege zur Republik 1945-1947, 2. Aufl., München, S. 301-338.

Weber, Jürgen, 1982: Auf dem Weg zum Grundgesetz. Von der Londoner Konferenz zum Parlamentarischen Rat, in: Jürgen Weber (Hg.): Entscheidungsjahr 1948, 2. Aufl., München, S. 71-114.

Weber, Jürgen, 1986: Der Westen formiert sich. Deutsche Soldaten auf der Tagesordnung, in: Jürgen Weber (Hg.): Die Bundesrepublik wird souverän. 1950-1955. München, S. 53-78.

Weidenfeld, Werner, 2011: Die Europäische Union. Unter Mitarbeit von Edmund Ratka, 2. Aufl., München.

Weidenfeld, Werner/ Wolfgang Wessels (Hg.), 2014: Europa von A bis Z. Taschenbuch der europäischen Integration, Bonn.

Wesel, Uwe, 1996: Die Hüter der Verfassung. Das Bundesverfassungsgericht, seine Geschichte, seine Leistungen und seine Krisen, Frankfurt a.M.

Wessels, Wolfgang, 2008: Das politische System der Europäischen Union, Wiesbaden.

Ziegelmayer, Veronika, 2001: Sozialstaat in Deutschland: Ein Systemwechsel?, in: Katrin Kraus/ Thomas Geisen (Hg.): Sozialstaat in Europa. Geschichte, Entwicklung, Perspektiven, Wiesbaden, S. 63-88.

Zohlnhöfer,/ Thomas Saalfeld (Hg.), 2015: Politik im Schatten der Krise. Eine Bilanz der Regierung Merkel 2009-2013, Wiesbaden.

Über den Autor

Martin Sebaldt, Prof. Dr. phil. habil., geboren 1961 in Bad Reichenhall. 1988 Magisterexamen, 1991 Promotion und 1996 Habilitation. 1997 Wissenschaftspreis des Deutschen Bundestages. Seit 2003 Inhaber des Lehrstuhls für Vergleichende Politikwissenschaft (Schwerpunkt Westeuropa) der Universität Regensburg. Nach zahlreichen Wehrübungen in der Gebirgstruppe, im Bundesministerium der Verteidigung und an der Führungsakademie der Bundeswehr Oberst der Reserve.

Wichtigste Publikationen: Die Thematisierungsfunktion der Opposition. Die parlamentarische Minderheit des Deutschen Bundestags als innovative Kraft im politischen System der Bundesrepublik Deutschland, Frankfurt a.M. u.a. 1992; Organisierter Pluralismus. Kräftefeld, Selbstverständnis und politische Arbeit deutscher Interessengruppen, Opladen 1997; Transformation der Verbändedemokratie. Die Modernisierung des Systems organisierter Interessen in den USA, Wiesbaden 2001; Verbände in der Bundesrepublik Deutschland. Eine Einführung, Wiesbaden 2004 (mit Alexander Straßner); Die Macht der Parlamente. Funktionen und Leistungsprofile nationaler Volksvertretungen in den alten Demokratien der Welt, Wiesbaden 2009; Pathologie der Demokratie. Defekte, Ursachen und Therapie des modernen Staates, Wiesbaden 2015; Nicht abwehrbereit. Die Kardinalprobleme der deutschen Streitkräfte, der Offenbarungseid des Weißbuchs und die Wege aus der Gefahr, Berlin 2017.